Our Ageing Population

Series Editor: Cara Acred

Volume 311

273 180

Independence Educational Publishers

First published by Independence Educational Publishers

The Studio, High Green

Great Shelford

Cambridge CB22 5EG

England

© Independence 2017

Copyright

Photocopy licence

The material in this book is protected by copyright. However, the
purchaser is free to make multiple copies of particular articles for instructional
purposes for immediate use within the purchasing institution.
Making copies of the entire book is not permitted.

ISBN-13: 978 1 86168 761 6

Printed in Great Britain

Zenith Print Group

Contents

Introduction

Our Ageing Population is Volume 311 in the **ISSUES** series. The aim of the series is to offer current, diverse information about important issues in our world, from a UK perspective.

ABOUT TITLE

The world's population is ageing; ever-more impressive medical advancements mean people are living longer than they ever have before. This, however, brings its own challenges. *Our Ageing Population* explores the changes society needs to make in order to properly care for its elderly citizens. It also looks at topics such as pensions, retirement age and care homes. Finally, it considers medical issues, age discrimination and loneliness in old age.

OUR SOURCES

Titles in the **ISSUES** series are designed to function as educational resource books, providing a balanced overview of a specific subject.

The information in our books is comprised of facts, articles and opinions from many different sources, including:

⇨ Newspaper reports and opinion pieces

⇨ Website factsheets

⇨ Magazine and journal articles

⇨ Statistics and surveys

⇨ Government reports

⇨ Literature from special interest groups.

A NOTE ON CRITICAL EVALUATION

Because the information reprinted here is from a number of different sources, readers should bear in mind the origin of the text and whether the source is likely to have a particular bias when presenting information (or when conducting their research). It is hoped that, as you read about the many aspects of the issues explored in this book, you will critically evaluate the information presented.

It is important that you decide whether you are being presented with facts or opinions. Does the writer give a biased or unbiased report? If an opinion is being expressed, do you agree with the writer? Is there potential bias to the 'facts' or statistics behind an article?

ASSIGNMENTS

In the back of this book, you will find a selection of assignments designed to help you engage with the articles you have been reading and to explore your own opinions. Some tasks will take longer than others and there is a mixture of design, writing and research-based activities that you can complete alone or in a group.

Useful weblinks

www.acas.org.uk

www.ageinternational.org.uk

www.channel4.com

www.communitycare.co.uk

www.theconversation.com

www.demos.co.uk

www.esrc.ac.uk

www.huffingtonpost.co.uk

www.ilcuk.org.uk

GOV.UK

www.theguardian.com

www.kcl.ac.uk

www.kingsfund.org.uk

www.mintel.com

www.nhs.uk

www.ons.gov.uk

www.telegraph.co.uk

FURTHER RESEARCH

At the end of each article we have listed its source and a website that you can visit if you would like to conduct your own research. Please remember to critically evaluate any sources that you consult and consider whether the information you are viewing is accurate and unbiased.

Our ageing world, in statistics

⇨ Today, 901 million people are over 60. [1]

⇨ 62% of people over 60 live in developing countries; by 2050 this number will have risen to 80%. [2]

⇨ Over the last half century, life expectancy at birth has increased by almost 20 years. [3]

⇨ It is estimated that by 2050 there will be over two billion people aged 60 and over, more than twice the number measured in 2000. Almost 400 million of them will be aged 80+. [4]

⇨ 80% of older people in developing countries have no regular income. [5]

⇨ Only one in four older people in low-and-middle-income countries receive a pension. [6]

⇨ 26 million older people are affected by natural disasters every year. [7]

⇨ The prevalence of disability among persons under 18 years is 5.8%; among 65- to 74-year-olds, the rate increases to 44.6%; the rate climbs to 84.2% among people aged 85 and over. [8]

⇨ Nearly two-thirds of the 44.4 million people with dementia live in low- or middle-income countries. [9]

Sources:

1. UN, Department of Economic and Social Affairs Population Division; World Population Prospects, key findings & advance tables; 2015 revision.

2. World Bank; Old Age Security and Social Pensions; page 2.

3. UNDESA World Population Ageing; 1950 – 2050; chapter 1: Demographic determinants of population ageing; page 6.

4. World Health Organization; 10 facts on ageing and the lifecourse (2012); pop up box pages 1, 2, and 3.

5. World Health Organization; Older persons in emergencies: considerations for action and policy development; page 11.

6. Global AgeWatch Index 2014, Insight Report, HelpAge International, 2014.

7. Cambridge Scholars; Rebuilding Sustainable Communities with Vulnerable Populations after the Cameras Have Gone; page XXI.

8. CODI; Age, Sex, Disability.

9. Alzheimer's Disease International; Dementia statistics.

⇨ The above information is reprinted with kind permission from Help Age International. Please visit www.ageinternational.org.uk for further information.

© Help Age International 2017

Is the UK really the best place in the world to die?

***An article from* The Conversation.**

THE CONVERSATION

By Tony Walter, Professor of Death Studies, University of Bath and Erica Borgstrom, Research Fellow, London School of Hygiene & Tropical Medicine

The UK has been given first place in the Economist Intelligence Unit's (EIU) *2015 Quality of Death Index*, which ranks palliative care across the world. This is the second time in a row that the UK has taken out the top spot – it topped the last index in 2010. The report attributes the UK's success to its comprehensive national policies, the integration of palliative care into the NHS, a strong hospice movement and deep community engagement.

Yet based on experience, we know that many deaths in the UK have been poorly managed. Hundreds of frail elderly patients died prematurely at the Mid-Staffordshire hospital. The Liverpool Care Pathway – intended to improve patients' last hours – came under fire for degenerating into a tick-box exercise – where staff seemed more concerned with meeting guidelines than administering appropriate care – and was abandoned. Low-wage staff in elderly 'care' are employed on contracts that leave them no time to go beyond performing the minimum care tasks mandated. And the health service ombudsman is disturbed by the regularity of complaints received about poor end-of life-care.

An EIU spokesperson said that there is still work to do in the UK, such as "ironing out occasional problems with communication or symptom control". But we believe the problems go much deeper.

The UK's palliative care services – which take a holistic approach to caring for a person's physical, mental and spiritual needs – are indeed excellent. But they are based on experiences with cancer care, when in fact more of us will die, not of cancer, but of multiple conditions – often including dementia – in an extended, vulnerable, frail old age.

This results in a very different kind of dying, often implicated in care scandals. So although the UK's palliative care services are excellent, the quality of death can still be poor for many citizens – particularly for those who aren't dying of cancer. And while, when comparing Britain's care services with the rest of the world, the EIU counted how many doctors and nurses have palliative care training, it did not take into account the factors that have led to bad deaths in the UK.

There is clearly a disconnect between the services provided in palliative care and the needs of many people dying in the UK. This confusion can be seen in the way we think and talk about end-of-life care. Our recent paper on this topic analyses how language defines reality and how policy interacts with scandal.

Compassion vs choice

The Government's 2008 *End of Life Care Strategy* for England was peppered with the word "choice". The strategy assumed that to get the kind of death they want, people need to talk about their preferences with their family and doctor.

But again, the strategy was based on expertise with cancer dying – where people often have full cognitive and communicative capacity and face a fairly predictable last few months. In fact, choice at the end of a very long life may be limited by the person's body and mind, by family relationships and by healthcare bureaucracies whose workings are opaque to patients – and even to those working within them.

Almost immediately after the strategy was released, Mid-Staffs and other care scandals broke. They highlighted not a lack of choice, but poor care. 'Care' has become a package to be bought, sold and delivered, rather than a quality of relation between care givers and receivers. And this 'bodywork' package is not always fully delivered: scandals cite service users not being given food or drink, not being taken to the toilet when needed, not turned over in bed.

So, in the wake of the care scandals, a new term was added to the healthcare lexicon. Media and politicians suddenly began talking about the need for "compassionate care": this means caring about the person, not just caring for their body.

Bridging the gap

If 'choice' is promoted by healthcare marketeers on the offensive, then 'compassion' is a defensive reaction to scandal – the default mantra of those trying to defend the NHS and social care. Following Mid-Staffs, the palliative care lobby continued to promote 'choice' as key to a good experience of dying, even though more choice would not have prevented the tragedy. Meanwhile, the media, the Royal College of Nursing, and Sir Robert Francis (tasked to investigate Mid-Staffs) promoted the need for 'compassion'.

For some years, the 'compassionate care' and 'choice' discourses continued in parallel, without much relation to each other. But now, they are getting back in touch. The 2015 Review of Choice in End of Life Care – mandated by the Coalition government and conducted by experts in palliative care – finally admitted that "good care necessarily involves choice and choice is valuable only when there is a foundation of good care".

Both "choice" and "compassion" approaches face limits and challenges when it comes to caring for those dying in old age. As it stands, we have yet to find a path forward at the middle ground. Some policy actors are beginning to see this. Extending access to palliative care from cancer to other conditions entails rethinking what choice and care mean. The challenge is much bigger than simply "ironing out occasional problems with communication".

12 October 2015

⇨ The above information is reprinted with kind permission from *The Conversation*. Please visit www.theconversation.com for further information.

How does getting older change the way we feel about our lives?

People aged 90 and over reported the lowest average feelings that activities they do in life are worthwhile.

ONS figures show that as people pass 75 years old they report decreasing levels of happiness, life satisfaction, and a sense of what they do in life is worthwhile.

But, those in the oldest age groups reported the lowest levels of anxiety, compared with younger age groups, although these levels remained unchanged beyond retirement age.

"As people pass 75 years old they report decreasing levels of happiness, life satisfaction, and a sense of what they do in life is worthwhile"

People aged 90 and over still reported higher life satisfaction and happiness than those in their middle years.

The findings help to inform an ongoing debate about how the UK can support an ageing population and focus on those things most important to a good later life.

The figures also found that people aged 65 to 79 tended to report the highest average levels of personal well-being people aged 65 to 79 tended to report the highest average levels of personal well-being.

How personal well-being is measured

Since 2011, ONS has asked people how they feel about their lives as part of a much wider initiative in the UK, and internationally, to look beyond traditional measures of progress and to measure what really matters to them.

The four measures which are used to monitor personal well-being in the UK are:

⇨ life satisfaction

⇨ sense that what one does in life is worthwhile

⇨ happiness

⇨ anxiety.

Why it is important to look at the well-being of older people

We're living longer and one in three babies will live to see their 100th birthday, according to latest estimates.

In 2014 there were more than half a million people aged 90 and older living in the UK, almost triple the number 30 years ago.

"People aged 65 to 79 tended to report the highest average levels of personal well-being"

But greater longevity can mean more complex health and social care needs, something which needs to be factored into Government policies and services.

3 February 2016

⇨ The above information is reprinted with kind permission from the Office for National Statistics. Please visit www.ons.gov.uk for further information.

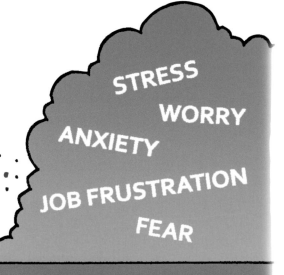

STRESS
WORRY
ANXIETY
JOB FRUSTRATION
FEAR

So nice to leave all that behind!

How has life expectancy changed over time?

In 1841 the average newborn girl was not expected to see her 43rd birthday. Thankfully times have changed and so have life expectancies in the 170 years since the first life table was constructed.[1]

The information contained in the Decennial Life Tables release, produced every ten years, provides a fascinating insight into those changes, spanning three centuries.

In 2011 life expectancy at birth is almost double what it was in 1841

Life tables calculate the number of years a person is expected to live given that they have already reached a certain age. For example, a girl born in 2011 is expected to reach age 82.8; however, someone who was 60 years old already in 2011 was expected to live a further 25.2 years, that is until that are 85.

A newborn boy was expected to live to 40.2 in 1841, compared to 79.0 in 2011, whereas a baby girl was expected to live to 42.2 in 1841 and 82.8 in 2011.

The low life expectancies of the 19th century can be explained by the higher number of infant deaths. Survival past the first year of life was historically a predominant factor in life expectancies and once a child had reached five years of age, he or she was much more likely to reach a greater age.

Whereas a newborn boy was expected to live to age 40.2 in 1841, a one-year-old boy in that same year had a life expectancy of 46.7 years – 6.6 years higher than a newborn.

Historically infant deaths were a major factor in life expectancies

In the 1840s around 15% of babies died before their first birthday compared with 0.4% in 2011, demonstrating the vast improvements made in reducing infant mortality.

The additional life expectancy of a one-year-old compared with a newborn continued to increase from 1841 to 1891; at its peak there was a difference of 8.1 years for boys and 6.8 years for girls.

This may have been due to the fact that it was not a legal requirement to register births until 1874, so data prior to this may have been less accurate (Births and Deaths Act 1874).

There has been a steady decline since the early 20th century, because of the improvements in public hygiene, childhood immunisations and the creation of the NHS (1948).

Females have consistently had a higher life expectancy than males… but the gap in 2011 is almost twice what it was in 1841

Female life expectancy at birth was 3.8 years higher than for men in 2011, compared to 2.0 years in 1841

This smaller gap in the mid-19th century was in part due to diseases and high infant mortality that affected men and women indiscriminately.

In the late 18th and early 19th centuries the gap between male and female life expectancies began to slowly widen, peaking at 6.3 years in 1971. It has been narrowing since, due to faster improvements in mortality for men than for women.

As well as men's working conditions being a factor, the widening gap can be explained by the decline in tuberculosis (TB). Deaths from the disease, which had been rife in the 17th and 18th centuries, and affected women more than men, had begun to decline in the 19th and 20th centuries. In the 20th century more women were surviving childbirth and were having fewer children, reducing their risk of dying in labour.

Since the 1970s, men have been catching women up in terms of survival. The decline of the mining industry and the move away from physical labour and manufacturing industries towards the service sector is a likely cause, along with a reduction in the proportion of men smoking.

Life expectancy at older ages continues to increase meaning our pensions need to last longer

The life expectancy of a woman aged 65 in 1841 was 11.5 years and reached 20.9 years in 2011. For men of the same age it was 10.9 years in 1841 and 18.3 years in 2011. But how has this affected how long pensions need to last?

In 1908, when the State Pension was first introduced for those aged 70 and over, a woman of this age was expected to live on average an additional 9.3 years, and a man 8.4 years (1901), meaning pensions needed to last around nine years. However, compare this to the latest figures and we see how pensions need to last longer. The current state pension age for men is 65 and for women it will reach 65 by November 2018. In 2011, men and women at this age were expected to live for approximately 20 more years, meaning we need to make our pensions last more than twice as long as when they were first introduced.

Footnote

Most life tables span more than one year; however, for ease of use this article uses the census year as the point of reference for each life table. For example, life table 3 spans from 1838 to 1854 but 1851 is used to plot life expectancy.

9 September 2015

⇨ The above information is reprinted with kind permission from the Office for National Statistics. Please visit www.ons.gov.uk for further information.

Why is it more difficult than ever for older people to leave hospital?

Discharging older patients from hospital, *the National Audit Office (NAO) report published today, focuses primarily on those patients deemed "medically fit for discharge" but who are stranded in hospital.*

By David Oliver

The NAO report looks beyond the official data on delayed transfers of care at the underlying issues affecting this group of patients.

Between 2013 and 2015, official delayed transfers of care rose 31 per cent and in 2015 accounted for 1.15 million bed days – 85 per cent of patients occupying these beds were aged over 65. The NAO estimates that the real number of delays is around 2.7 times higher than those officially counted. No wonder delayed discharges topped the list of concerns reported by NHS finance directors in The King's Fund's latest *Quarterly Monitoring Report.*

Waiting for social care was the biggest cause of this sharp rise. Since 2010, waits for home care packages have doubled and waits for beds in nursing homes increased by 63 per cent. This isn't surprising given the increasing number of old, frail and medically complex hospital patients, coupled with ten per cent cuts in real-terms funding for social care over the past five years. The Barker Commission warned of the potential impact on the NHS of inadequate social care funding and the anomaly between free-at-point-of-use health care versus means-tested and highly rationed social care.

But it's not just social care. The NHS Benchmarking National Audit of Intermediate Care estimates that we only have around half the intermediate care places we need nationally, and that average waits for home care rehabilitation and re-ablement are now eight and six days, respectively. And as money gets tighter, delays caused by waiting for decisions on NHS-funded continuing care are increasingly problematic.

The NAO's conclusions on cost are particularly interesting: it estimates that the current cost of delays to the hospital sector is £820 million per annum, compared to a hypothetical cost of alternative community services for all those patients of just £180 million. This potential saving is a scenario based on all those delays being remedied, and requiring activity or capacity to be taken out of acute beds at a time when they are pressurised. Recent history would suggest caution in making such projections.

So what's the solution? The NAO makes a series of recommendations, but here I will make some suggestions of my own. Let's take the need for adequate funding capacity for both social care and community health services for granted. These are usually the same services that can support people outside hospital and prevent admissions in the first place. For instance, the intermediate care audit has shown that rapid response teams providing 'wrap around' services in people's own homes can prevent hospital admissions in precisely the group of patients most likely to end up delayed. Several examples of this integrated care approach were showcased at our conference earlier this year and in our 2014 report.

Some delays are simply down to poor collaboration, poor information-sharing and clunky procedures at the interfaces between hospitals and local partners. Mistrust between professionals can also be an issue. Or even worse, current financial constraints mean that it may be in their interests to introduce delays in order to delay spending. Trusts such as Sandwell have reduced delays by moving towards one point of access, telephone referral, single trusted assessment and one team.

Finally, it's important that acute hospitals also deliver solutions, for example, by addressing variability in bed occupancy, minimising internal delays for investigation or treatment and repeated ward moves. Senior decision-makers and specialist teams at the hospital door; rapid access ambulatory care clinics; specialist frailty assessment units; and a relentless focus on rehabilitation, discharge planning, senior review and real-time use of data on delays can help to reduce bed occupancy and get more patients straight back home on being declared medically fit for discharge. Hospitals can also reduce the need for step-down services by maximising patients' independence. Case studies from Sheffield and Warwickshire have shown what can be done. The NAO and NHS Benchmarking reports have shown that a growing number of hospitals have embraced these approaches but their application is still variable.

With a mounting acute provider sector deficit of £2.45 billion and £8.7 billion more savings to come, concerted action on delayed transfers of care is essential to avoid worsening performance on meeting urgent care targets. But most of all, delays impose a huge human cost on real people with real families and real concerns marooned in hospital. How easily we can lose sight of this.

26 May 2016

⇨ The above information is reprinted with kind permission from The King's Fund. Please visit www.kingsfund.org.uk for further information.

Age discrimination

The Equality Act 2010 makes it unlawful to discriminate against employees, job seekers and trainees because of age. For example, this may include because they are "younger" or "older" than a relevant and comparable employee.

Key points

There are four main types of age discrimination.

Direct discrimination

Breaks down into three different sorts of direct discrimination of treating someone 'less favourably' because of:

⇨ their actual age (direct discrimination)

⇨ their perceived age (direct discrimination by perception)

⇨ the age of someone with whom they associate (direct discrimination by association).

Direct discrimination because of someone's actual age is the only one of the three different sorts of direct discrimination that may be objectively justified as what the law terms "a proportionate means of achieving a legitimate aim". This means it must be proportionate, appropriate and necessary (economic factors such as business needs and efficiency may be legitimate aims).

Indirect discrimination

Can occur where there is a policy, practice, procedure or workplace rule which applies to all workers, but particularly disadvantages people of a particular age. For example, a requirement for job applicants to have worked in a particular industry for ten years may disadvantage younger people. In some limited circumstances, indirect discrimination may be justified if it is "a proportionate means of achieving a legitimate aim".

Harassment

When unwanted conduct related to age has the purpose or effect of violating an individual's dignity or creating an intimidating, hostile, degrading, humiliating or offensive environment for that individual.

Victimisation

Unfair treatment of an employee who has made or supported a complaint about age discrimination.

Age discrimination rights apply to the vast majority of workers, including 'office holders', police, barristers and partners in a business. Under the Act, limited exceptions regarding age can be allowed in some areas. They can include pay and other employment benefits based on length of service. There are also some limited exceptions and exemptions relating, for example, to the National Minimum Wage, redundancy payments, insurance and pensions.

The Act says there are no upper age limits on unfair dismissal and redundancy.

Employers should ensure they have policies in place which are designed to prevent age discrimination in:

⇨ recruitment

⇨ determining pay, and terms and conditions of employment

⇨ training and development

⇨ selection for promotion

⇨ discipline and grievances

⇨ countering bullying and harassment

⇨ when an employee is dismissed.

Making a claim of age discrimination

If someone feels they have been discriminated against, they may be able to make a claim to an employment tribunal. However, it's best to talk to the employer first to try to sort out the matter informally, in order to minimise the negative effects on all parties involved.

Claimants who wish to bring a claim or appeal to a tribunal will have to pay a fee. An initial fee will be paid to issue a claim and a further fee will be payable if the claim proceeds to a hearing. There are two levels of fee which will depend on the type of claim. Further information is available from Ministry of Justice – Employment Tribunal guidance.

Through the Acas Helpline you can get free advice on specific problems and alternatives to a tribunal claim, such as Mediation or Early Conciliation, where appropriate.

Retirement

Employers cannot force employees to retire or set a retirement age unless it can be objectively justified as "a proportionate means of achieving a legitimate aim". To find out more, see the Acas web page on Retirement.

⇨ The above information is reprinted with kind permission from Acas. Please visit www.acas.org.uk for further information.

"Work till you drop" warning on pensions

Some people may have to work till they are 81 to build up a decent pension pot, according to a report.

With the Government carrying out a review of the state pension age, research from Royal London says an average earner who starts saving for an occupational pension at 22, and makes the minimum statutory contributions, would need to work until 77 if they want the sort of "gold standard" pension enjoyed by their parents.

Royal London defines this "gold standard", which includes the state pension, as two thirds of pre-retirement income.

For those living in high-income areas, such as Westminster and Wandsworth in London, achieving a pension pot of this size would take till 80 or 81, assuming contributions are not increased.

At the same time, a review for the Labour party has concluded that employees should double their contributions to workplace schemes, with a target of 15 per cent of earnings going into pension pots.

Traditionally, the state pension age was 65 for men and 60 for women.

This is being equalised and in two years' time it is due to rise, reaching 67 by 2028.

This could rise again as a result of a government review, amid warnings that those starting work today could have to wait until their mid-70s before they receive a state pension.

Royal London's research shows that how much people need to save in occupational schemes, if they want a "gold standard" pension, varies according to where they live.

Variations

While someone in Westminster who makes minimum monthly contributions would have to wait till they are 81, a worker in Boston, Lincolnshire, where incomes are lower, would build up a big enough pot by 73.

Ages for Scotland, Wales and Northern Ireland are 77, 76 and 76, respectively.

Former pensions minister Steve Webb, who is director of policy at Royal London, said: "It is great news that millions more workers are being enrolled into workplace pensions, but the amounts going in are simply not enough to give people the kind of retirement they would want for themselves, and certainly not the sort of pensions that many of those retiring now are enjoying.

"Even in lower wage areas, people face working into their early seventies to get a comfortable retirement. In higher wage areas, the state pension makes a much smaller contribution, so workers in those areas face working well into their seventies."

Mr Webb said the answer was to start saving early and increase pension contributions.

2 March 2016

⇨ The above information is reprinted with kind permission from *Channel 4 News*. Please visit www.channel4.com for further information.

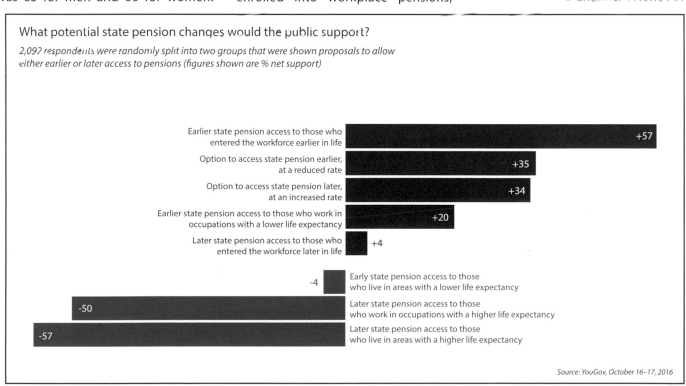

What potential state pension changes would the public support?

2,092 respondents were randomly split into two groups that were shown proposals to allow either earlier or later access to pensions (figures shown are % net support)

- Earlier state pension access to those who entered the workforce earlier in life: +57
- Option to access state pension earlier, at a reduced rate: +35
- Option to access state pension later, at an increased rate: +34
- Earlier state pension access to those who work in occupations with a lower life expectancy: +20
- Later state pension access to those who entered the workforce later in life: +4
- Early state pension access to those who live in areas with a lower life expectancy: -4
- Later state pension access to those who work in occupations with a higher life expectancy: -50
- Later state pension access to those who live in areas with a higher life expectancy: -57

Source: YouGov, October 16–17, 2016

A turbulent history of British pensions, since 1874

From a five-shilling payment for men over 70 to George Osborne's reforms, **Telegraph Money** *charts the eventful history of pensions past.*

By Teresa Hunter

The road to our brave new world of pensions has been a rocky one. Paved with best intentions, the journey ended, sadly too often, in scandal, u-turns and empty promises – potholed by political meddling and rising life expectancy.

For some, those days are over. Ros Altmann, the Government's older workers' tsar, believes we have finally arrived at our destination – a modern, user-friendly retirement solution, fit for the 21st century.

But leading commentator Tom McPhail of Hargreaves Lansdown is more ambivalent. He fears the speed of reform will ignite a bonfire, making more change inevitable.

He said: "One thing I am sure of is that this is just the beginning. There will be more change, although it is hard to say what that will be. Many good things will come out of the reforms. Some people will make mistakes. Where we go next, I really don't know."

Other experts believe that rather than scaling new horizons we are, in many ways, turning the clock back.

Deborah Cooper, a senior partner at the actuarial firm Mercers, said: "In some ways we have come full circle. If you go back 100 years, the first pensions were paid to people aged 70 and over, to keep them from starving. Future generations may have to wait until 70 to get their state pension, and it will provide only a basic level of sustenance."

We take a look at the seven ages of pensions, what has been achieved, the growing pains – and what went wrong.

First Age: beginning of the journey

Technically pensions are thought to date back to Roman times; centurions received an 'annuity' when their days of active service were over. But anything we would recognise as a modern pension is barely 100 years old, and like Shakespeare's infant, came 'mewling' into the world.

The first 'old age' pension was introduced by the Government in 1908, paying five shillings a week (worth around £14 today). At a time when the average life expectancy was 47, it was only available to men aged over 70.

Shortly before this, embryonic workplace pensions took shape. In 1874, we saw the first nurses' pension paying £15 annually to "broken down" carers, followed by a more comprehensive National Pension Fund for Nurses in 1887.

Schemes covering civil servants, teachers and police were set up in the 1890s. Railway companies were the first industrialists to offer pensions, followed by Reuters in 1882, WH Smith in 1894 and Colmans in 1899.

Coverage, though, remained thin, until the 1921 Finance Act introduced tax relief on pension contributions. This was followed, in 1925, by a skeleton contributory state pension scheme for male manual workers who were earning less than £250 a year. It paid a total of ten shillings weekly (around £15 today) from the age of 65.

It was not until 1940, after the outbreak of the Second World War, that women joined the party.

The Old Age and Widows' Pension Act introduced a pensionable age of 60 for unmarried women who paid in, and widows of insured men.

Second Age: pensions start to grow up

The modern universal compulsory state pension did not arrive with its 'shining morning face' until 1948. The 1942 Beveridge Report envisaged a social insurance scheme, designed not to provide a comfortable income in retirement, but a safety net against destitution.

However, as a report from the Institute of Fiscal Studies (IFS) points out, the insurance-based system envisaged by Beveridge was never implemented, because it could not provide for the millions of older workers, many of whom had fought in two world wars. It failed to offer them sufficient time to build up a fund for themselves.

So, instead, the 'pay as you go' system we have today was introduced, whereby today's contributions pay today's pensions.

An IFS spokesman said: "Over time, the link between a person's contributions and their own pension has become even weaker."

Third Age: heyday of hope and expectation

During the following quarter of a century, pensions, like most other things, boomed. The post-war shortage of manpower led firms to increasingly offer attractive company pensions to retain managerial and skilled staff.

However, Chris Noon, a senior partner at Hymans Robertson, the pensions consultancy, points out that these were only promises and not guarantees. He said: "It was a kind of 'best endeavour, we'll try our best' environment. Indeed, it was similar to the 'defined ambition' world that the pensions minister, Steve Webb, would like to see reintroduced."

High inflation, interest rates and stock market returns saw the value of pension funds soar, with many apparently hatching large surpluses which started to attract the attention of politicians.

But accounting rules and overall supervision at the time were weak.

Ms Altmann said: "Were the surpluses real? They weren't necessarily real in the same way deficits may not be real today. No one knows. That's the point with pensions, they are paid out a very long time in the future.

"These were young schemes started in the Fifties and Sixties. They didn't begin to pay out in any serious way, until decades later, when all of the problems materialised."

By 1967, more than eight million employees working for private companies enjoyed a final salary pension, along with four million state workers.

In 1978, the Labour Government introduced a fully fledged "earnings-linked" state top-up system for those without access to a company scheme.

Fourth Age: dawning of reality

As the funds became richer, they became more powerful and the question of who owned them was more pressing. Employers had considered the funds their own private domain, with freedom to pay pensions to whom they pleased, if and when they pleased.

Many staff were discriminated against. Employees who left the company paid heavily in penalties. Part-timers and contract workers were not allowed to join.

Increased regulation became inevitable. In 1985, companies were forced to inflation-proof the pensions of leavers, and in 1989, schemes were obliged to pay men a pension at the same age as women, following the famous Barber legal battle. Part-timers and other excluded staff had to be offered benefits.

All this pushed up costs.

At the same time, the Government became concerned about the future bills that the State Earnings-Related Pension Scheme (SERPS) was ratcheting up. The Thatcher Government introduced a widespread package of reform in 1988. The power of the company to control the labour market was broken, and individuals were given the right to not join their employer's scheme. Similarly, individuals could contract out of SERPS into a private pension and the Government paid them attractive incentives for doing so.

Fifth Age: the wheels start to come off

The Nineties began with a loud splash when newspaper baron Robert Maxwell fell off his yacht, leaving his publishing empire on the brink, only to reveal that he had stolen £400 million from the Mirror Group pension scheme.

Suddenly pensions had become headline news, as was their lack of supervision. The public clamoured for increased protection of their pension savings.

Sixth Age: the era of scandal

It wasn't long before the Thatcher reforms turned sour, when in 1993 it emerged that some unscrupulous

financial advisers had been mis-selling personal pensions to earn fat commissions. This triggered payments of more than £11 billion to six million people caught up in a mis-selling scandal.

There was worse to come.

Seventh Age: the collapse

It started to emerge that the industry, while in some cases overestimating potential investment returns, had consistently underestimated life expectancy, which was growing sharply.

Instead of a year or two of leisure after work, pensioners were increasingly enjoying a quarter of a century of good health. And they expected generous pensions to fund it.

The sums didn't add up, and many schemes collapsed. Strong employers, who could afford their promises, also pulled up the drawbridge. Today only around a million working in private industry have access to a final salary pension.

Public sector pensions were also reformed, yet around five million state employees continue to enjoy a salary-linked pension.

The Pension Protection Fund was established in 2004 to bail out collapsing funds. However, it is paid by a levy on other funds, adding to their burden.

The state pension, too, was under pressure, so the Government first increased the female pension age to 65, and to 66 for anyone currently in their late fifties, rising to 67 for those in their mid-fifties.

The Chancellor, George Osborne, linked the state pension age to rising longevity, implying younger generations will have to work until they are 70 to get a state pension – just like their Edwardian great-grandfathers.

From 2016, everyone will receive the same basic "level" pension of around £7,500 annually. At the same time, quasi-compulsory workplace contributions have been introduced through the auto-enrolment system.

The future

Is this the final act of what Shakespeare might have called "this strange eventful history"?

We have the prospect of an adequate basic state pension, a flexible system of private savings, with an element of compulsion.

The key dates

- ➾ Late 19th century beginning of occupational pensions
- ➾ 1908 first 'old age' pension paid by the Government
- ➾ 1921 Finance Act introduces tax relief for pension contributions
- ➾ 1924 voluntary contributory pension is brought in for those who could afford to save
- ➾ 1948 the modern state pension is introduced under the Beveridge Report
- ➾ 1978 state earnings-linked top-up (SERPS) was provided

- ➾ 1985 pension funds had to increase payments to company leavers
- ➾ 1988 Thatcher pension reforms
- ➾ 1989 Barber judgement ruled pension ages must be equal between men and women
- ➾ 1991 Maxwell pension scandal pushed pensions on to the front page and up the political agenda
- ➾ 1993/4 pensions mis-selling scandal
- ➾ 2004 Pension Commission set up to investigate private pensions under Lord Turner of Ecchinswell
- ➾ 2010 state pension age for women starts to rise from 60 to 65
- ➾ 2012 auto-enrolment begins for big employers

- ➾ 2012 new universal flat-level pension is announced for all
- ➾ 2014 March budget announces new freedoms to cash in your pension
- ➾ 2015 freedom and choice regime begins
- ➾ 2016 new flat-rate state pension to be launched.

9 April 2015

- ➾ The above information is reprinted with kind permission from *The Telegraph*. Please visit www.telegraph.co.uk for further information.

75 is the new 65, so we should all keep working for longer

An article from **The Conversation.**

THE CONVERSATION

By Warren Sanderson, Professor of Economics, Stony Brook University (The State University of New York) and Sergei Scherbov, Deputy Director of World Population Program, International Institute for Applied Systems Analysis (IIASA)

The idea of raising the retirement age is not popular – most people resent being told they must work for longer. But with life expectancies increasing and people enjoying higher quality of life at older ages, we face the prospect of older people being retired for the same amount of time as they were working, or longer.

"With life expectancies increasing and people enjoying higher quality of life at older ages, we face the prospect of older people being retired for the same amount of time as they were working, or longer"

Our research supports the decision to raise retirement ages, but also shows how we can stop relentlessly raising retirement ages by maximising the workforce available in younger generations.

According to conventional thinking, pension ages have to go up because there is not enough money in national budgets to continue the current level of benefits that pensioners receive. This is a very unpopular argument and for good reason.

If the desired policy was to maintain a constant pension age, then there are many ways to do this, from reducing less valuable programmes to increasing the efficiency of government services or raising taxes. Increasing pension ages simply because pension programmes are growing more expensive is like deciding that students should have less education because schooling is becoming more expensive.

But, a continuation of current demographic trends suggests that 75-year-olds in the future could have the same remaining life expectancy, health, and other characteristics of today's 65-year-olds. When we realise this, it seems appropriate to modify the normal pension age in order to not encumber younger generations with an ever heavier burden of supporting their elders.

Flexibility is key

But retirement age should not just be uniformly raised. We cannot tell whether populations are ageing or not just by looking at the fraction of people over the age of 65. We must examine the characteristics of people, and policies should be made accordingly.

Pension payments are normally adjusted for price changes. What is needed is some form of flexibility of the retirement age that takes into account changing life expectancies. If life expectancy is longer, retirement should be later and vice versa if shorter – there is no need for an arbitrary figure that determines when everyone should retire.

We would broadly agree with the Australian Government's recent decision to raise the retirement age to 70, to take into account the fact that their life expectancy is now 85. But this shouldn't necessarily be implemented across the board.

> ## "A continuation of current demographic trends suggests that 75-year-olds in the future could have the same remaining life expectancy, health, and other characteristics of today's 65-year-olds"

To allow for this flexibility, it's important to increase the number of people working who are able to do so. Our research indicates that a one to two percentage point increase in the average number of people working can spread the burden of tax across working adults and allow one year to be taken off the normal pension age.

This can be done through eliminating arbitrary restrictions that mean people have to leave the labour force when they would actually like to carry on in their jobs, supporting the retraining of older workers, helping people with young children remain employed, changing disability rules so that partially disabled people can work while receiving some benefits and through many other policies.

Increasing the number of people working this way is not only good for the economy, but would prove popular too by giving people jobs who want them.

Policy challenge

As older people live longer and become healthier, the policy challenge is to give them the flexibility of being productive as long as they wish. Reducing restrictions on people who would otherwise want to work is a win-win policy. It provides people with more options and, at the same time, it reduces the need for large increases in the pension age.

Policy debates miss two important elements when it comes to increasing pension ages. First, they do not have to make the poor worse off if benefits are adjusted at the same time. Second, increases in pension ages should not be addressed in isolation.

Increasing the number of people working through other measures should be done at the same time. A better way to discuss pension age increases is to address it in the context of finding the best policy mix, involving pension ages, labour force participation and the progressiveness of the pension benefit schedule.

Healthily ageing populations

The debate over retirement ages is often framed in the context of coping with the challenges of an ageing population. But, despite the numerous graphs showing skyrocketing fractions of populations above the age of 65, we have to question the idea that populations are ageing. The problem with these graphs is that they categorise everyone as 'old' when they reach their 65th birthday.

But 65-year-olds half a century ago are not the same as they are today, nor are today's 65-year-olds the same as they will be half a century hence. 65-year-olds in the future will live longer, be healthier, and more educated than they are now. This is good news. But we need not get in a panic about ageing populations and implement the policies to reflect them.

21 Nay 2014

⇨ The above information is reprinted with kind permission from *The Conversation*. Please visit www.theconversation.com for further information.

Here's what people in their 90s really think about death

An article from **The Conversation.**

By Jane Fleming, Senior Research Associate, University of Cambridge

THE CONVERSATION

Across the developed world more people are living longer, which of course means more get to be extremely old by the time they die. Nearly half of all deaths in the United Kingdom are in people aged 85 or older, up from only one in five just 25 years ago.

Dying in older age can mean a different sort of death, such as becoming gradually frailer in both body and mind and developing numerous health problems over many years. Where years after retirement were previously considered just old age, a longer life span means the later years now include variation reflected in labels such as younger old and older old.

Our previous research showed people who are over 90 when they die need more support with daily life in their last year than even those who die in their late 80s. In the United Kingdom, around 85% of those dying aged 90 or older were so disabled as to need assistance in basic self-care activities. Only 59% of those between 85 and 89 at death had this level of disability.

This knowledge has implications for planning support for life and death in different care settings. But what do we know about what the older old (95 plus) people actually want when it comes to decisions about their care as they approach the end of their lives?

How the older old feel about dying

The oldest and frailest in our society are becoming less visible as many who need the most support, such as those with dementia, are either in care homes or less able to get out and about. But their voices are crucial to shaping end-of-life care services.

In our latest research, we had conversations about care experiences and preferences with 33 women and men aged at least 95, some over 100, and 39 of their relatives or carers. Of these, 88% were women, 86% were widowed and 42% lived in care homes.

Death was part of life for many of the older people who often said they were taking each day as it comes and not worrying too much about tomorrow. "It is only day-from-day when you get to 97," said one woman. Most felt ready to die and some even welcomed it: "I just say I'm the lady-in-waiting, waiting to go," said one.

Others were more desperate in their desire to reach the end. "I wish I could snuff it. I'm only in the way," was a typical sentiment in those who felt they were a nuisance. Others begged not to be left to live until they were 100, saying there was no point to keeping them alive.

Most were concerned about the impact on those left behind: "The only thing I'm worried about is my sister. I hope that she'll be not sad and be able to come to terms with it."

The dying process itself was the cause of most worries. A peaceful and painless death, preferably during sleep, was a common ideal. Interviewees mainly preferred to be made comfortable rather than have treatment, wishing to avoid going into hospital.

We found families' understanding of their relative's preferences only occasionally incorrect (just twice). For instance, one person said they wanted to have treatment for as long as they could, while their family member believed they would prefer palliative care. This highlights the importance of trying to talk options through with the older person rather than assuming their family knows their views.

We found most discussed end-of-life preferences willingly and many mentioned previous talk about death was uncommon, often only alluded to or couched in humour. A minority weren't interested in these discussions.

We need to talk with the older old

It's rare to hear from people in their tenth or eleventh decade but there are some studies that have explored the views of the younger old. Most often these have concentrated on care home residents and occasionally on those living at home.

A literature review conducted in Sweden in 2013 found a total of 33 studies across the world that explored views of death and dying among older people, although very few of these sought the views of the older old.

A 2002 study found older people in Ghana looked forward to death, seeing it as a welcome visitor that would bring peace and rest after a strenuous life. And a 2013 study in The Netherlands showed many people changed their preferences on how they wanted to die as their care needs changed.

A recent review examined older people's attitudes towards advance care plans and preferences for when to start such discussions. It identified 24 studies, mainly from the United States and with younger old age ranges. The results showed that while a minority shirked from end-of-life care discussion, most would welcome them but were rarely given the opportunity.

These studies support our findings on older people's willingness to discuss often taboo topics, their acceptance of impending death, and their concerns around what the dying process would bring: increasing dependence, being a burden and the impact of their own death on those left behind.

To plan services to best support rising numbers of people dying at increasingly older ages in different settings, we need to understand their priorities as they near the end of life.

19 May 2016

⇨ The above information is reprinted with kind permission from *The Conversation*. Please visit www.theconversation.com for further information.

More men than women in the sandwich generation provide day-to-day help for their parents

⇨ **Within the Sandwich Generation, 71% of men say they maintain the well-being of their parents or their partner's parents compared to 65% of women**

⇨ **Overall, 39 % of this generation say they've had to take time out of work to look after their parents, their partner's parents, or their children in the past 12 months**

⇨ **72% say they try to find activities that they, their parents and their children can do together**

With the population of over-65s continuing to grow and the average age of women having their first child also rising, a growing number of people are coming under pressure to care for and support not only their offspring, but also their ageing parents, as well as holding down employment. Within this 'Sandwich Generation'[x], new research from Mintel shows that seven in ten (68%) say they give day-to-day help to their parents or their partner's parents and almost a third (30%) offer financial help.

Notably, whilst stereotypically it is the women of the family who provide care to elderly parents, Mintel's research shows that amongst the Sandwich Generation, men are more likely to take an active role. Of UK adults who support both parents and children, 71% of men say they maintain the well-being of their parents or their partner's parents compared to 65% of women, whilst a third (32%) of men say they provide financial help compared to just over a quarter (27%) of women.

What is more, whilst some 96% of mums take care of children when sick compared to 26% of dads, almost half (45%) of men in the Sandwich Generation take their parents or their partner's parents to medical appointments compared to a third (33%) of women.

Jack Duckett, Consumer Lifestyle Analyst at Mintel, said:

"Today's parents are increasingly under pressure to care for and support not only their offspring, but also their ageing parents whilst holding down employment; leaving them 'sandwiched' between generations. As adults falling into the Sandwich Generation are only set to increase in number as the population continues to age, this generates multiple opportunities for companies and brands to help provide assistance and support for families under pressure. The high level of involvement that men have when it comes to looking after their parents or their partner's parents can be attributed to women largely retaining responsibility for caring for their own children."

Mintel's research also reflects the time-pressed nature of this generation, with three-quarters (76%) of 'Sandwichers' currently in employment and 51% claiming they don't have much free time for themselves, rising to 61% of those aged 35–44. In addition, two in five (39%) of this generation say they've had to take time out of work to look after their parents, their partner's parents, or their children in the past year.

Consequently, over a quarter (27%) of this generation indicate they would be interested in greater workplace flexibility and 23% indicate they would like more healthcare advice about how to look after ageing parents. Interest in receiving support for helping children move out of the family home is also high, with one in five (19%) 'Sandwichers' expressing interest in initiatives designed to help children fly the nest.

"Whilst children may grow up and flee the nest eventually, the rapid increase of older adults is only likely to put more pressure on today's Sandwich Generation; after all, the oldest demographics will continue to require ever more levels of care in coming years. This makes it crucial for brands and companies to look to support carers, particularly through the development of new technologies and services that will help to ease their lifestyles and provide them with some much-needed 'me-time'," Jack comments.

One major benefit to arise from the time pressures put on Sandwich Generation adults is the amount of time their children often get to spend with their grandparents. Indeed, three-quarters (76%) of Brits in the Sandwich Generation say their children spend some of their free time with their grandparents and 72% say they try to find activities that they, their parents and their children can do together.

"As the Sandwich Generation grows, providing additional support to those caring for both children and parents, as well as providing them with opportunities to take time out for themselves, will be essential. There is huge value to be found in helping these multi-generational family structures enjoy time together, as it allows them not only to build strong emotional bonds but also to share important life-skills," Jack concludes.

*The Sandwich Generation ('Sandwichers') is defined by this report as adults aged 30+ who are responsible both for bringing up their own children and for the care of their ageing parents.

25th March 2015

⇨ The above information is reprinted with kind permission from Mintel. Please visit www.mintel.com for further information.

'Not enough over-50s' taking aspirin to prevent heart disease

"Aspirin a day could dramatically cut cancer and heart disease risk… study claims," *the* Mail Online *reports.*

US researchers ran a simulation of what might happen if all Americans over 50 years old took aspirin on a daily basis. Their results found that people would live about four months longer on average, adding 900,000 people to the US population by 2036.

The study was designed to demonstrate the possible long-term effects of more people taking aspirin to prevent cardiovascular disease.

It should be pointed out that there is an important difference between UK and US guidelines. In the UK, low-dose aspirin is usually recommended for people with a history of heart disease or stroke. In the US this advice is extended to people who are at risk of cardiovascular disease but don't have it yet.

We already know that aspirin reduces the risk of heart disease and strokes caused by blood clots (ischaemic stroke). There's some evidence it may reduce some types of cancer. However, aspirin also increases the risk of stroke caused by bleeding (haemorrhagic stroke) and increases the chances of bleeding in the stomach or gut.

So should you be taking low-dose aspirin? Without knowing your individual circumstances it is impossible to provide an accurate response. You need to ask your GP.

Where did the story come from?

The study was carried out by researchers from the University of Southern California and a company called Analysis Group. The authors received no funding for the study.

The study was published in the peer-reviewed journal *PLOS One*, on an open-access basis so it's free to read online.

The *Mail Online* reports the study as if the findings about aspirin reducing cardiovascular disease and potentially extending lifespan were new, while they have actually been known for some time.

The report says taking aspirin "would save the US $692 billion in health costs," which seems to be a misunderstanding. Health costs would actually increase, because of people living longer.

However, the researchers assigned a value of $150,000 to each additional year of life lived, which is how they arrived at the $692 billion figure.

What kind of research was this?

This was a "microsimulation" study, which used a modelling system to project possible outcomes under different scenarios, using information from health surveys. This type of modelling can throw up some interesting possibilities, but because it relies on so many assumptions, we have to be cautious about taking the results too literally.

What did the research involve?

Researchers used data from cohort studies to predict average life expectancy, cardiovascular events, cancers, disabilities and healthcare costs for people in the US aged 50 and over. They predicted what would happen with the current numbers of people taking aspirin, then with everyone currently recommended to take aspirin doing so, then with everyone over 50 taking aspirin.

Deaths from cardiovascular disease and numbers living with cardiovascular disease (CVD)			
Nation	Number of people dying from CVD (latest year)	Number of people under 75 years old dying from CVD (latest year)	Estimated number of people living with CVD
England (2015)	129,147	33,622	5.9 million
Scotland (2015)	15,768	4,655	670,000
Wales (2015)	9,027	2,544	375,000
Northern Ireland (2015)	3,733	1,087	225,000
United Kingdom (2015)	158,155	42,245	7 million+

Source: Deaths BHF/Oxford from latest official statistics (ONS/NISRA/NRS 2015 data); UK total includes non-residents (ONS data). Living with CVD estimates based on latest health surveys with CVD fieldwork and GP patient data.

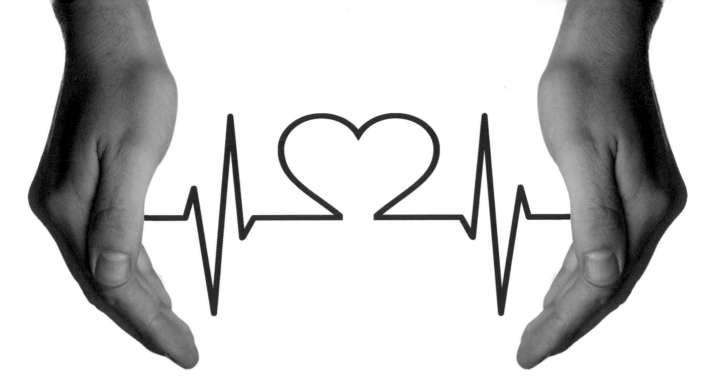

They compared the results of their modelling, to see what effect it would have on average lifespan, the US population, costs and benefits.

Cohort studies providing data included the National Health and Nutrition Examination Survey (NHANES), Health and Retirement Study of Americans, Medical Expenditure Panel Survey and Medicare Current Beneficiary Survey.

The model included an assumption that more people would have gastrointestinal bleeding as a result of taking aspirin. It also modified the results using quality of life measures, so that additional life years were adjusted for quality of life.

What were the basic results?

The researchers found that, if everyone advised by US guidelines to take aspirin did so, the:

⇨ numbers of people with cardiovascular disease would fall from 487 per 1,000 to 476 per 1,000 (11 fewer cases, 95% confidence interval (CI) -23.2 to -2)

⇨ numbers with gastrointestinal bleeding would rise from 67 per 1,000 to 83 per 1,000 (16 more cases, 95% CI 3.6 to 30)

⇨ years of life expectancy at age 51 would rise from 30.2 years to 30.5 years, an additional four months of life (0.28 year, 95% CI 0.08 to 0.5)

⇨ life expectancy without disability would rise from 22.8 years to 22.9 years, an additional one month of life (0.12 year, 0.03 to 0.23).

The model found no reduction in the numbers of strokes or cancers.

The model shows there could be an additional 900,000 people (CI 300,000 to 1,400,000) alive in the US in 2036, who would otherwise have died.

Using the figure of $150,000 per quality-adjusted life year to represent benefits, the researchers say the value of extra life gained by 2036 would be $692 billion.

How did the researchers interpret the results?

The researchers said: "Expanded use of aspirin by older Americans with elevated risk of cardiovascular disease could generate substantial population health benefits over the next 20 years, and do so very cost-effectively."

Conclusion

This study doesn't really tell us anything we didn't already know. Aspirin has been used for many years to prevent heart attacks and strokes in people with cardiovascular disease. Aspirin's wider use is controversial, because of the potential side effects.

What this study does add is an estimate of what might happen if all people in the US who were advised to take aspirin under US guidelines, actually did so. (The researchers say that 40% of men and 10% of women advised to take aspirin don't take it.)

The study assumes that people would get the same benefits as those seen in clinical trials of aspirin. This is unrealistic, because most studies find that people tend to do better in clinical trials than when being treated in the real world.

The average results – showing an additional one month of disability-free life for every 1,000 people – may sound trivial. However, it's important to remember that averages don't work like that in real life. Many people will get no benefit from aspirin, while a smaller group will avoid a heart attack or stroke, and so live many more months or possibly years, as a result of taking aspirin.

If you've already had a heart attack or stroke, or if you have angina or another heart or circulation problem, your doctor has probably prescribed low dose aspirin. There's good evidence that aspirin (or similar drugs, for those who can't take aspirin) can help prevent a second heart attack or stroke.

1 December 2016

⇨ The above information is reprinted with kind permission from NHS Choices. Please visit www.nhs.uk for further information.

Getting ready for ageing: a manifesto for action

An extract from the report by the Ready for Ageing Alliance.

Foreword

The world's population is ageing rapidly. This is true of our country too. Projections suggest this means:

⇨ 51% more people aged 65 and over in England in 2030 compared to 2010.

⇨ 101% more people aged 85 and over in England in 2030 compared to 2010.

By 2021, there will be around one million people living with dementia in the UK and by 2051 this will have reached 1.7 million, more than double the number in 2012

Another result of this demographic trend is that around one-third of babies born in 2013 in the UK are expected to celebrate their 100th birthday.

These changes will impact on our society and economy, for every kind of organisation and for each individual.

To take just three examples: a growing older population is a big new potential market for companies, provided they understand and can meet older people's needs and desires for products and services; the health and care system clearly has to adapt to people living longer and with multiple long-term conditions like dementia, diabetes, hypertension and arthritis; and as individuals we are likely to need more savings to see us past retirement.

We need to start taking serious action now. The longer we leave it, the more difficult the process of adaptation will be and the greater the numbers of ordinary people who will needlessly suffer. This manifesto sets out the actions that should be embarked on now

What we have to stop doing or reverse

Stop seeing ageing as being about older people: ageing is about all of us. It isn't about young versus old. We will fail to tackle the challenges and make the most of the opportunities of ageing whilst we pitch one generation against another.

Stop ignoring the demands and needs of an ageing population: in Government there is not and never has been a minister, senior official or other post holder such as a 'Commissioner' or 'Tsar', or any cross-cutting unit or government strategy on an ageing society.

Stop delivering communities which fail to deliver beyond the basics: Sadly, many communities are even failing to provide the basics of public toilets and places to rest. A fear of falling and of crime acts as a barrier to getting out and about for many older people. We must deliver a more ambitious vision for our communities: of places which are fun and engaging for all ages, whilst also reducing the risk of isolation and loneliness.

End the discrimination: age discrimination remains a barrier to the participation of older people

in society. Legislation has gone some way to prevent discrimination but policymakers must ensure that older people are not prevented from accessing products and services simply because of their age. We all need to play a part in normalising ageing.

Reverse the decline in new and appropriate housing stock for older people: the numbers of new retirement homes being built are being allowed to fall at the same time as the numbers of older people are rapidly increasing. Too few new homes are being built. Those which are, are too often not accessible or adaptable for old age.

Stop ignoring the crisis in social care: government investment in social care is sharply shrinking while the numbers of older people who need it are rising, yet good social care saves public money by reducing and postponing older people's need for expensive acute hospital care and helps them to live independently for longer. Good social care for older people also allows family members to keep in employment – so they are not forced to choose between work and caring for an older relative.

Stop operating hospitals on a model designed for the past: hospitals of the 21st century are increasingly made up of older patients with complex needs. Staff ratios on hospital wards dedicated to older people, many of them with dementia, are typically lower than those in general wards. Yet we know that these older people often have greater need of help with essentials like eating and drinking.

Stop under-utilising older people: the over-65s in the UK currently spend around £2.2 billion per week (£114 billion per annum) on goods and services. Assuming the spending of the 65+ population rises in line with annual inflation of 2%, their spending will reach over £6 billion per week by 2037. People aged 65 and over in the UK last year contributed £61 billion to the economy through employment, informal caring and volunteering. Yet almost four in ten workers aged 55–64 are not working. And almost half of the unemployed of this age range are in long-term unemployment. We must do more to maximise the social and economic contribution of older people.

Ensuring our communities are ready for ageing

Local authorities should ensure that their community development plans take account of the ageing society. They need to plan communities to be places which contribute to improving the quality of life and tackling loneliness amongst people of all ages.

Community development approaches have much to teach us about the contribution of relationships and social connectedness. Investment in these types of approaches can help prevent problems of loneliness and social isolation in later life at a relatively low cost. The creation of dementia-friendly communities is one example where we've seen real local action towards helping people living with the condition live well.

Initiatives to get people walking and cycling should focus on all ages, not just younger people. Public transport must be safe, accessible, reliable and affordable for all ages.

The voluntary sector must make the most of the opportunity an ageing society brings whilst also developing its services to meet an older consumer with complex needs and wants. The sector should better understand the diversity of the ageing experience and respond to the challenges set out by the Commission on the Voluntary Sector and Ageing.

Anti social behaviour and fear of crime are big issues for many older people. Addressing them can help them to get out and about.

Action is necessary to increase the supply of housing, including retirement housing, to make it easier for older people to move to properties more suitable to their changing needs if they wish to do so.

All newly constructed homes should comply with "lifetime home design standards" so that future generations of older people can live in them safely and comfortably for much longer.

Early installation of home aids and adaptations, like grab-rails, should be incentivised, for example by encouraging local authorities to lower the means-test threshold for accessing them, as they are a cost-effective way of supporting older people to live independently at home.

Leaseholders should have access to good, impartial information and advice and to an effective system for complaints and redress; this would be especially helpful to older people living in sheltered and some other forms of retirement housing.

We need a genuinely level playing field in terms of planning law and practice to support the development of more retirement housing.

Ensuring you are ready for ageing?

⇨ Get fit: keeping physically active is one of the most important things we can do to ensure a healthy old age. Learn to ride a bike or get out to the park. Not everyone can do a marathon, but most of us should keep fitter than we do.

⇨ Save for your old age: yes, you will get a state pension. But for most people, it is unlikely to provide the sort of income you are used to. Saving is important at any age. But the younger we start, the greater we benefit from investment returns and compound interest.

⇨ Pay off your debts: having debt can be a major barrier to preparing for ageing.

⇨ Get advice from a charity such as Age UK or Stepchange and start planning for the future.

⇨ If you smoke, stop or cut down: smoking reduces our life expectancy and can make it more likely that we suffer poor health or need care in old age. You are never too young or old to stop.

⇨ Be healthy: eat a healthy balanced diet, drink enough water, and not too much alcohol. Be mentally active. Keep yourself informed about how you can prevent ill health and ask your GP if you need any adult vaccinations.

22 August 2014

⇨ The above information is reprinted with kind permission from ILC-UK. Please visit www.ilcuk.org.uk for further information.

© Ready for Ageing Alliance 2017

Gene linked to youthful appearance may help solve ageing puzzle

***An article from* The Conversation.**

THE CONVERSATION

By Richard Faragher, Professor of Biogerontology, University of Brighton

How long you live depends in part on the genes you inherit. For example, those suffering from Werner's syndrome have inherited two defective copies of a gene coding for an enzyme that is involved in DNA replication and repair.

A lack of this enzyme produces premature cell senescence – the build up of dysfunctional cells as we age which causes damage to tissue – and elevated levels of inflammatory proteins. The end result is the early development of many conditions seen in older people, such as cardiovascular disease, osteoporosis, grey hair, wrinkled skin and shrinkage of the thymus. Werner's syndrome is perhaps the nearest thing we will ever see to true accelerated ageing.

At the other end of the scale are individuals who carry rare variants of the Foxo3a gene who show high physical and cognitive function late in life, as well as lower incidences of some age-related diseases and better self-reported health. Those fortunate enough to carry two copies of one of these rare variants have roughly three times the average chance of living into their late nineties. In essence, Foxo3a and wrn variants determine the biological age of those who carry them.

Genes and perceived age

In contrast, a new study published in *Current Biology* reports the first genetic variants to influence how old those who carry them are perceived to be by others. Groups of four observers estimated the facial age and percentage of facial skin covered by wrinkles in more than 2,600 mainly white Dutch participants in their mid-60s (an average of about 1.3% of skin was wrinkly). Reassuringly, the real age of the subjects correlated strongly with how old the investigators thought they looked and, perhaps unsurprisingly, the more wrinkled the face the older the observers guessed the person was.

A study entitled "scientists discover that wrinkled people look quite old" would hardly have made headlines. However, after investigating the genomes of the participants, the researchers discovered that changes in a gene known as MC1R were strongly associated with perceptions of facial age. People unfortunate enough to inherit two defective MC1R variants (including those which cause red hair and pale skin) were rated by the observers as being about two years older than people whose MC1R genes were working properly. Those who inherited one "good" variant and one "bad" one looked about a year older. So the gene could successfully explain why some guesses were off.

This is the latest discovery of a gene involved in ageing. For example, a study published earlier this year showed that the gene IRF4 is involved in the greying of hair by helping to regulate the production and storage of melanin. It is clear that some of these "ageing genes" have major effects on health while others' influence is a little more aesthetic – which makes them far from unimportant.

Evolutionary importance

So just what is MC1R doing? It could just be cosmetic, but this gene carries the information for a receptor which plays a key role in the synthesis of melanin (which blocks UV light) and prevents inflammation – a major driver of ageing. Defective forms of this can in fact predispose someone to skin cancer.

Why could this matter? Genes have to be passed from one generation to the next. Over a billion years ago there was selection for any genetic variation which allowed early organisms to reproduce more successfully than their competitors even if these genes led to decreased survival later on.

This Faustian bargain, known as "antagonistic pleiotrophy", is all that ageing is.

However, in more evolved species, the situation is complicated by sex. Mates have to be selected, attracted and sometimes kept which results in competition both between members of the same sex and between sexes. This process influences ageing because, depending on the species, the process of either competing for a mate or being the object of competition can shorten lifespan. For example, female fruit flies that mate regularly have shortened lifespans due to the damaging effects of chemicals that male flies secrete to destroy the sperm of previous mates.

It is now recognised that humans also (albeit subconsciously) follow evolutionary drivers in mate selection and retention. Human males typically desire youth in partners more strongly than females do (because female fertility declines much more sharply with age). Given this context, carrying a gene variant that accidentally makes you look even older than you really are (or worse which truthfully advertises your above average propensity to skin cancer) is hardly an advantage, especially if you are a woman.

On the plus side, across 37 different cultures one of the top three most strongly desired traits in a long-term partner for both sexes is kindness. There are probably genes for that as well, but it is at least independent of wrinkles.

29 April 2016

⇨ The above information is reprinted with kind permission from *The Conversation*. Please visit www.theconversation.com for further information.

Researchers develop novel test which can tell how well a person is ageing

The findings, published today in *Genome Biology*, could help improve management of age-related disease by identifying people most at risk of diseases affected by age, as well as improve the way anti-ageing treatments are evaluated.

The seven-year collaborative study at King's College London, Karolinska Institutet in Sweden and Duke University in the US, used a process called RNA-profiling to measure and compare gene expression in thousands of human tissue samples. Rather than looking for genes associated with disease or extreme longevity, the Medical Research Council (MRC)-funded researchers discovered that the 'activation' of 150 genes in the blood, brain and muscle tissue were a hallmark of good health at 65 years of age. The researchers were then able to create a reproducible formula for 'healthy ageing', and use this to tell how well a person is ageing when compared to others born the same year.

The researchers found an extensive range in 'biological age' scores of people born at the same time indicating that a person's biological age is separate and distinct to his or her chronological age.

Importantly, a low score was found to correlate with cognitive decline, implying that the molecular test could translate into a simple blood test to predict those most at risk of Alzheimer's disease or other dementias and suitable for taking part in prevention trials.

A person's score was not, however, found to correlate with common lifestyle-associated conditions, such as heart disease and diabetes, and is therefore likely to represent a unique rate of ageing largely independent of a person's lifestyle choices.

The researchers say their findings provide the first practical and accurate test for the rate at which individual bodies are ageing. If this is the case, it could lead to numerous insights in research because 'age' is a critical factor in almost every area of medicine.

At the same time, the molecular test could enable more suitable donor matching for older organ transplants and could also provide a more efficient way of determining if an animal model of ageing is suitable to evaluate the effectiveness of anti-ageing treatments.

However, the study does not provide insight into how to improve a person's score and thus alter their 'biological age'. While a low score could be considered as 'accelerated ageing', an important aspect of the work suggests that ageing does not now need to be defined only by the appearance of disease.

Lead author of the study, Professor James Timmons at the Division of Genetics and Molecular Medicine at King's College London, said: "Given the biological complexity of the ageing process, until now there has been no reliable way to measure how well a person is ageing compared with their peers. Physical capacity such as strength or onset of disease is often used to assess 'healthy ageing' in the elderly but in contrast, we can now measure ageing before symptoms of decline or illness occur.

"We now need to find out more about why these vast differences in ageing occur, with the hope that the test could be used to reduce the risk of developing diseases associated with age."

Dr Neha Issar-Brown, programme manager for population health sciences at the MRC added: 'Whilst it is natural for our bodies and brains to slow down as we age, premature ageing and the more severe loss of physical and cognitive function can have devastating consequences for the individual and their families, as well as impact more widely upon society and the economy.

"This new test holds great potential as with further research, it may help improve the development and evaluation of treatments that prolong good health in older age."

This research was funded by the Medical Research Council, the Innovative Medicines Initiative (EU/EFPIA), the Wallenberg Foundation and the National Institutes of Health.

7 September 2015

⇨ The above information is reprinted with kind permission from King's College London. Please visit www.kcl.ac.uk for further information.

Brain training improves memory and performance of everyday tasks in older people

Playing online games that challenge reasoning and memory skills – brain training – could have significant benefits for older people in their day-to-day lives, according to a new study published today (3 Nov) in JAMDA.

Researchers at the Institute of Psychiatry, Psychology & Neuroscience (IoPPN) at King's College London have shown that an online brain training package can not only improve memory and reasoning skills – but also how well older people carry out everyday tasks such as navigating public transport, shopping, cooking and managing personal finances.

Previous research has shown some promise for brain training in improving memory, although these small-scale studies have been inconclusive. This new research, which is funded by Alzheimer's Society, is the largest randomised control trial to date of an online brain training package. Involving almost 7,000 adults aged over 50, it is also the first to evaluate the impact of computerised brain training on how well people can perform their daily activities.

The brain training package comprised three reasoning tasks, such as balancing weights on a see-saw, and three problem-solving tasks, such as putting numbered tiles in numerical order. Study participants (initially recruited from the general population through a partnership between the BBC, Alzheimer's Society and the Medical Research Council) were encouraged to play the game for ten minutes at a time, as often as they wished. Before starting the study and again after six weeks, three months and six months, the participants completed a series of cognitive tests, including measures of grammatical reasoning and memory. Those over 60 were also assessed on a test of daily living (e.g. using the telephone, navigating public transport and doing the shopping).

After six months, brain training led to significant improvements in scores on the test of daily living in people over 60, and significant improvement in reasoning and verbal learning in those over 50 compared to those who didn't play the reasoning and problem-solving games. Playing the brain-training games five times per week was most effective in bringing about these improvements.

While some decline in memory and thinking skills is a normal part of healthy ageing, more severe impairments can be a precursor to dementia, a condition characterised by the progressive loss of ability and function. Previous research has shown that people who have complex occupations or engage in cognitively stimulating activities such as crosswords, puzzles and learning new skills throughout life tend to have lower rates of dementia.

This new study could have important implications for preserving cognitive function in older adults and might offer an effective, easily accessible intervention to help people reduce their risk of cognitive decline later in life.

Dr Anne Corbett from the Wolfson Centre for Age-Related Diseases at the Institute of Psychiatry, Psychology & Neuroscience (IoPPN), King's College London, said: "The impact of a brain-training package such as this one could be extremely significant for older adults who are looking for a way to proactively maintain their cognitive health as they age. The online package could be accessible to large numbers of people, which could also have considerable benefits for public health across the UK.

"Our research adds to growing evidence that lifestyle interventions may provide a more realistic opportunity to maintain cognitive function, and potentially reduce the risk of cognitive decline later in life, particularly in the absence of any drug treatments to prevent dementia."

Dr Doug Brown, Director of Research and Development at Alzheimer's Society said: "Online brain training is rapidly growing into a multi-million pound industry and studies like this are vital to help us understand what these games can and cannot do. While this study wasn't long enough to test whether the brain-training package can prevent cognitive decline or dementia, we're excited to see that it can have a positive impact on how well older people perform essential everyday tasks.

"With a rapidly ageing population, evidence that this type of brain training has a tangible, real-life benefit on cognitive function is truly significant. As government and society explore ways to enable people to live independently as they get older, this study has important implications for policy makers and public health professionals.

"Finding ways to help people maintain good brain health and avoid dementia is a key focus for the Society's research programme and we're delighted to be funding the next stage of this research. We need as many people over 50 to sign up to help us test the effect of brain training over a longer time period."

Dr Corbett added: "Today we're launching a new open trial to see how well older people engage with the brain-training package over the long term. We want to investigate how genetics might affect performance to allow us to better understand how brain training could be used to maintain cognition or even reduce the risk of cognitive decline and dementia."

Dr Anne Corbett is supported by the NIHR Biomedical Research Centre and Dementia Unit at the South London and Maudsley NHS Foundation Trust and King's College London.

3 November 2015

⇨ The above information is reprinted with kind permission from King's College London. Please visit www.kcl.ac.uk for further information.

"Why we need to make elder abuse an imprisonable offence"

Action on Elder Abuse head Gary FitzGerald explains why the charity has launched a campaign for new laws to protect abused older people.

The abuse of older people is routinely recognised as a major issue, not just in the UK, but in many countries across the world. Both the United Nations and the European Union have developed statements and policies aimed at generating awareness and action by member states, and there are widely differing but proactive approaches being taken to address it. Nevertheless it continues to be a growing cause for concern.

The number of older people in the UK is set to rise significantly, to around 19 million in just over 30 years, with an increasing number of 'very' old people. The 2007 *UK Study of Abuse and Neglect of Older People* identified that 8.6% of older people living in the community experience elder abuse (suggesting there will be 1.6 million victims by 2050, unless we make a significant impact on what is happening now). This is in addition to the abusive experiences of older people in hospitals and care homes, which appear to continue despite all the commitments to change and improvement.

Rising rates of abuse

In England, the proportion of referrals to adult protection concerning people aged over 65 rose from 60% to 64% from 2011–12 to 2014–15. Despite being asked by Action on Elder Abuse, both the Association of Directors of Adult Social Services and the Government have declined to initiate any information campaigns in response to this increase. Based on the prevalence study, Action on Elder Abuse estimates that no more than one in ten victims ever reach the attention of adult protection, so the situation is likely to be far worse in reality than current referral rates suggest.

The nations of the UK have adopted different approaches to adult protection legislation. While England, Scotland and Wales have all introduced legislation to put the "infrastructure" of adult protection on a statutory footing – notably through the creation of multi-agency boards or committees to oversee safeguarding – England has done little more than this. In Wales, and more so in Scotland, powers of entry or intervention have been introduced to help practitioners take action to tackle the abuse of vulnerable adults.

But all of these systems are focused on stopping any abuse that might be occurring, or about to occur, not on taking action against the perpetrator, other than curbing or restricting their actions if legal powers allow. The only acknowledgement of the criminal nature of abuse within adult protection is the expectation that the police will investigate possible crimes. Investigation however is different from prosecution.

Masking criminality

In reality, the terminology and philosophy of adult protection has masked the criminal nature of abusive acts. Calling an incident "physical abuse" instead of assault or actual bodily harm lessens its importance and impact. Calling something financial abuse instead of theft or fraud implies that it falls outside of the criminal justice process. And it becomes even easier to marginalise the impact if you can refer to it as "poor practice" in service provision and a "serious incident" in a hospital environment. Such an approach reduces the scale and cost of such crimes, because they are then no longer part of the criminal justice system, but it also provides no deterrence to future abuse and undermines the status of older people as equal citizens in our society.

Very few cases of elder abuse ever reach the courts. Statutory services will sometimes argue that this is because most older people do not want prosecution. It is true that, in some abuse situations, it is not in the victim's best interest to prosecute and they do not want to do so. However, while this is equally true in domestic abuse situations, there is a commitment from the criminal justice system to proceed with a prosecution even if the domestic abuse victim objects, where there is sufficient evidence and it is deemed in the public interest. Such an approach should apply equally to elder abuse.

Lack of convictions

And yet, the reality is that most elder abuse that could be prosecuted is not. It is either not considered an option, or it is addressed through a police caution, which is not a criminal conviction. One police force told AEA in response to a freedom of information enquiry that they had investigated 76 instances of elder abuse or neglect and had issued a police caution in every case, an action that seems highly dubious.

But even if a case of elder abuse gets to court it will very rarely result in a prison sentence for the perpetrator, regardless of the seriousness of the act or the impact on the victim. It is more likely to result in a suspended sentence or community service, neither of which can be considered a deterrent for future abusers.

All of which explains why it is time to draw a line under the current social policy approach to abuse and instead consider elder abuse to be an aggravated offence that carries statutory minimum sentencing. This would bring the UK in line with many other countries, including America, Japan and Israel.

Proposed offences

This is what we propose:

⇨ Any person who inflicts pain or suffering, including mental suffering, on an older person who is in their care and custody should be the subject of a charge of 'elder abuse'. It should be the responsibility of the accused to prove that such actions were not intentional or wilful. Anyone employed in the provision of either health or social care should in all instances be considered to have acted with intent in such situations, with the burden on them to prove differently.

⇨ Elder abuse would be punishable by imprisonment of up to four years. If in the commission of the offence, the victim suffers grievous bodily harm or death, the perpetrator should receive an additional jail term of five or ten years, respectively.

⇨ Any carer of an older person, or any person in a position of trust and confidence who steals from, or defrauds on older person of property or money, should be the subject of a deterrent sentence that is proportionate to the impact of the crime on the victim. Any person who uses a power of attorney to steal from or defraud an older person should be the subject of an increased sentence, reflective of the breach of trust.

⇨ Health practitioners, care providers and staff, clergy members, and employees of local authorities, statutory bodies, financial institutions and police should be required by law to report known or suspected cases of elder abuse to the relevant local authority/health and social care trust adult protection/safeguarding teams and to encourage the public in general to do so.

⇨ An older victim of elder abuse should be able to obtain a court order restraining an abuser from further acts of abuse, and this process should be simple and speedy.

⇨ Where there is reasonable suspicion that an older person is being subjected to elder abuse, and a third party denies access to see and speak to that older person, a police officer should be enabled to obtain a court order granting access.

Why only older people?

We have chosen to campaign for an offence in respect of older people specifically for two reasons: because that links with laws in other countries, showing such offences are possible and could be beneficial; and because we can draw substantially on our own data to make the case for older people in a way we could not for other groups. But we are not resistant to extending such a law to encompass other vulnerable adults, and would encourage this.

Of course, there will be those who will argue that we already have sufficient laws and we just need to make them work more effectively. But that does not address the additional aggravating factors of elder abuse, such as the frailty and vulnerability of victims and the increased impact upon them because of those factors. This was the same justification used for the introduction of aggravated offences for hate crime, under which offences are treated more severely if motivated or accompanied by hostility to a person based on their real or perceived membership of a racial or religious group, disability or sexual orientation.

There will also be those who will argue that such an approach belittles older people, because it somehow suggests that they cannot protect themselves. No one would suggest that the introduction of domestic abuse laws has undermined or belittled the status of women, or that the introduction of hate crimes have had a similar impact on people from minority communities. It is when we compare and contrast these attitudes and arguments with actions already taken in support of other parts of society that we truly perceive the extent to which an ageist approach allows the continuation of elder abuse. It has to stop. Now.

15 June 2016

⇨ The above information is reprinted with kind permission from Community Care. Please visit www.communitycare.co.uk for further information.

Kicking age discrimination into touch

Record numbers of older people are bringing their skills, talents and experience into the UK workplace.

Reaping the benefits of a fuller working life is 71-year-old Eddy Diget from Milton Keynes, who is believed to be the oldest fitness trainer in the UK.

The former Royal Navy worker, who has practised Chinese martial arts for 55 years, is currently training an array of gifted athletes including a British heavyweight cage fighter, a South African rugby player and competitive bodybuilders at DW Fitness club where he works full-time.

Kung-Fu master, Eddy, said:

"I haven't got any plans to slow down or retire soon. I'm extremely passionate about what I do and I'd probably do it for free! I enjoy being busy, and keeping active physically and mentally is good for you! Every day I'm passing on my years of experience to the younger fitness trainers and of course my clients – it is very rewarding.

"Companies that are reluctant to hire older people really are missing a trick. More mature people tend to be reliable, confident, organised, great listeners and, most importantly, have the experience of life. The latter can be priceless. With a quarter of the workforce aged over 50, UK older workers are leading the way in the workplace and the Government is committed to promoting the benefits of people staying in work."

Pensions Minister, Baroness Altmann, said:

"Getting older shouldn't mean you feel compelled to stop work. There are opportunities out there and employers are increasingly valuing the skills and experience of over-50s. Whether it is continuing a lifelong career for longer, training for an entirely new role or even moving to self-employment, don't write yourself off too soon.

"We know that people enjoy the social side of being in work and can enjoy fuller working lives. It is becoming normal for people to have more control over their career as we have outlawed forced retirement. A key part of my role as Pensions Minister is to challenge stereotypes and ageism in the workplace. Eddy is a brilliant example of the value older people can offer – it would certainly be a brave person to tell Eddy he should stop working and retire!"

Ross Simpson, Head of Leisure at DW Sports Fitness, said:

"In an industry that is traditionally dominated by younger people, the company has benefited from maintaining an open-minded and flexible approach to recruitment.

"The likes of Eddy bring so much valuable experience and know-how. By its very nature, the fitness industry is cyclical, with new trends and routines emerging all the time.

"Our older trainers are at a distinct advantage, as they've seen these fads come and go. They have a great understanding of what works and what doesn't, and this nous and experience rubs off on our younger employees. Additionally, we actively target older members and have a range of senior memberships, so it's important to have more experienced trainers who can connect with this demographic.

"It's also vital that youngsters who are just entering the field have mentors to look up to, especially when they're as committed, knowledgeable and passionate as Eddy."

More information

The UK has an ageing population, which offers both challenges and opportunities for individuals, businesses and the economy. By 2022 there will be 3.2 million more people aged between 50 and State Pension age, yet 200,000 fewer people aged 16 to 49.

The Age Action Alliance is an independent partnership of organisations, including the Department for Work and Pensions, that works together to take a collaborative approach to the challenges of an ageing society.

18 April 2016

⇨ The above information is reprinted with kind permission from GOV.UK.

© Crown copyright 2017

The future of the retirement home

By Eleanor Doughty

Think to the future and space age technology might well factor in on decisions made. In property, technological advancements have brought us underfloor heating and heating systems that can be controlled from hundreds of miles away.

But what is the future of the retirement home?

The number of those requiring such a property is ever increasing. By 2037, one in four of us will be over 65, compared to one in six at present.

As we live longer and government digs its heels in on building suitable affordable housing, one housing provider has produced its vision of what retirement housing will look like in the future.

Anchor's design for the new generation of retirement homes is tech-tastic. With rotating gardens and virtual pets, it envisages what retirement housing could look like in 50 years time.

Currently, retirement property makes up just two per cent of the UK's housing stock. Just one per cent of those in their 60s live in their retirement housing in the UK, compared to 17 per cent of the same age group in the United States. In the UK, this is mostly limited to the social rented sector: of the 500,000 or so retirement properties that exist, approximately 105,000 are available for sale. For homeowners who are reluctant to move into rented property after they retire, this presents a problem – a lack of supply of mid-market retirement housing, for those with modest levels of equity.

The generation of baby boomers at and approaching retirement own a substantial amount of housing wealth. An estimate by the think tank Demos in 2013 is that the over-60s own £1.28 trillion, of which £1.21 trillion is unmortgaged.

Anchor's property is cylindrical, and fully customisable. Glazed doors allow the indoor and outdoor spaces to intersect easily, and there are dedicated areas for virtual yoga classes, alfresco dining, and a vertical garden for all year round planting.

Research conducted by Anchor for the accompanying "Silver Chic" report found that there are four themes surrounding safe and secure retirement property. These are: comfort, connectivity, community, and financial and physical security.

This research found that the older generation are reluctant to move to retirement villages away from cities and towns. Most want to live in vibrant communities, but value their peace and quiet. Anchor dictates therefore that these properties of the future should be built in urban and suburban areas, providing easy access to local amenities. While space may be at the premium, Anchor's research suggests that a number of high-rise retirement properties may be necessary to supply the country with adequate appropriate housing.

"There are a number of significant issues facing the retirement sector in the coming decades and we will need new, innovative forms of retirement housing and care services to respond to these trends," said Howard Nankivell, Anchor's sales director.

"Good quality housing, that meets the needs of the end user, has huge potential to help people live happy and healthier lives, delaying the need to move from independent living into residential care. This in turn helps reduce the ever-increasing pressure of our ageing population on the NHS as well as unlocking valuable housing stock at the top end of the market."

12 January 2016

⇨ The above information is reprinted with kind permission from *The Telegraph*. Please visit www.telegraph.co.uk for further information.

Improving with age? How city design is adapting to older populations

By Alice Grahame

As cities experience a demographic shift, the need for age-friendly design is becoming ever more critical. From almshouses to driverless cars, the future of urban housing and mobility may just be shaped for and by the elderly.

There is no denying it: like it or not we are all getting older. According to the UN *World Population Prospects* report, the global population of older people is growing at an unprecedented rate. By 2050, for the first time in human history, there will be more over-65s than children under 15. The number of people over 100 will increase by 1,000%. And as by then 70% of the world's population will likely live in cities, this will present huge challenges, and cities will need to adapt.

Of course an ageing population is not inherently a bad thing: it reflects improved health and rising life expectancies. However, as we age,

our housing, transport and social needs change. By preparing for this, policymakers, town planners and architects can make it more likely that older populations can still lead fulfilling lives.

The global engineering firm Arup has looked at how authorities are responding to this demographic shift. Stefano Recalcati, project leader behind the firm's report *Shaping Ageing Cities*, explains that cities must adjust if older people are to maintain quality of life: "It's important to be conscious of the ageing trend. It is a huge challenge for world cities – they will need to change, to make sure older people continue to play an active role in the community and don't become isolated. Isolation has a negative impact on health so tackling that is really important."

"Small innovations can make a difference," Recalcati adds. "Older people are less likely to drive, favouring

public transport and walking. The average person over 65 manages a walking speed of 3km/hour. At 80 that goes down to 2km/hour, compared with the average for a working-age person of 4.8km/hour. Reducing the distance between transport stops, shops, benches, trees for shade, public toilets and improving pavements and allowing more time to cross the road all encourage older people to go out."

In the UK, the Government has just announced the building of ten new towns designed to address ageing and health issues such as obesity. As well as encouraging more active lifestyles, the designs could include wider pavements, few trip hazards and moving LCD signs, making the streets easier to navigate for people with dementia and other age-related conditions. London-based charity Living Streets has also been working alongside communities carrying out street audits with older residents to see what improvements could be made, as well as campaigning at a strategic level to influence positive legislative and infrastructure changes. Their project Time to Cross campaigned to increase pedestrian crossing times which resulted in Transport for London (TfL) agreeing to a review.

Cities that have addressed accessibility are likely to be ahead of the game in age-friendliness. In recent years there have been efforts to make cities more accessible to both disabled and elderly residents and visitors. Berlin is aiming for 100% accessibility by 2020. The city authorities are working to widen pavements, bring in tactile guidance at road crossings and easier access to trams and buses. This year Milan won the European Commission's Access City Award for its high standard of building design and access to transport.

What lessons can urban planners learn from looking at existing retirement communities? These are popular in the US and growing in other parts of the world: separate towns, often gated, for over-55s. Deane Simpson, an architect

who teaches at the Royal Danish Academy of Arts in Copenhagen, recently spoke at an event organised by Museum of Architecture and The Building Centre in London about designing cities for an ageing population. In his book *Young-Old: Urban Utopias of an Ageing Society*, Simpson looks at communities for 55- to 75-year-olds who are retired and in good health with money to spend. One scheme, The Villages in Florida, a network of 'village' developments housing 115,000 over-55s linked by a 90-mile network of car-free golf-cart roadways – offers a life of restaurants, bars, cinemas and sports.

Simpson is critical of the way this type of lifestyle cuts people off from the rest of society, with age becoming a new form of segregation. However, he accepts that they reflect a desire for an active, experience-filled lifestyle.

Simpson admits that there are certain elements that could be applied to a multigenerational urban setting: "The golf cart infrastructure provides a transport network for vehicles slower than cars. This could be replicated as a way of integrating mobility scooters and electric wheelchairs and bicycles. In Denmark and The Netherlands where biking culture is strong, bike lanes are increasingly being used by mobility scooters. It is a way of enabling safe mobility for those not able to walk and not able to drive."

The US model of retirement communities is increasingly being exported. In China more than a quarter of the population will be over 65 by 2050. The elderly have traditionally been taken care of by the extended family – often with three generations living together. But demographic changes are severely challenging

that family unit. The one child policy combined with longer life expectancy means that a typical married couple could be looking after four parents and up to eight grandparents.

There is a rise in assisted living schemes, like the US-designed Merrill Gardens in Shanghai and Harbin. Lead 8 is an architecture and design studio working in the region; their co-founder and director Simon Blore explains that they have worked on new developments in China that are 80–100% geared towards elderly groups. "We attempt to maintain the scale of a typical Chinese village; all needs are met within a short walking distance (the elderly in China do not have cars, and may no longer even use bicycles). Overlaid on this is a system of 'local' health clinics, essential services, open spaces and leisure facilities, which is not so different from assisted living housing, but on a much larger scale."

"In China more than a quarter of the population will be over 65 by 2050"

Blore has reservations about whether US-style senior living will be widely accepted: "I think most people want to be part of regular society, part of the community, so that's probably a challenge internationally – trying to get that balance right – a place with a high level of care and a sense of community and a relationship with the wider society."

Lead 8 is working on a Malaysian residential complex in Kelana Jaya, near Kuala Lumpur, that could offer a solution. "On each floor there are flats of different sizes next to each other, with a wall that can be taken down. An owner can buy two adjoining apartments – one large and one small. The family lives in the big one with grandparents next door, and they can either be separate or interconnect."

Integration rather than segregation is advocated by London architect Stephen Witherford. His firm, Witherford, Watson, Mann, will be building a complex of 57 flats for over-75s in Bermondsey, London. The project is based on the traditional almshouse model of charitable

housing for pensioners, but updated for the 21st century. "Traditionally almshouses were set back behind a fence," explains Witherford, "but we wanted to create a version that would tackle the problem of isolation. It will have a lounge that opens directly on to the high street." There will be a cookery school, performance space, rooftop allotment and a workshop. Residents can hold craft fairs, cake sales and perform or watch plays. "The public can come in and get involved. Amenities are nearby and there is a bus stop outside for trips into town." Rethinking traditional designs is also a priority for Susanne Clase, an architect with White Arkitekter, who is designing flats for seniors in Gothenburg, Sweden, and including potential residents and home-care professionals in the decision-making. She explains the flats are designed to accommodate regular visits from professional carers who help with personal tasks: "In our design the public and private spaces are reversed. The bedroom and bathroom are by the front door so the carer can access them. The living room and kitchen are at the back and are the resident's private space." Clase believes that designing with ageing in mind is good for everyone. "It's important to help people live independently for as long as possible, and to design that in from the beginning rather than make adaptations later on. We already have a high level of accessibility in Sweden. You won't get a permit to build unless you can show that if the resident breaks a leg it won't be a problem. So we are already thinking ahead."

"[China's] one child policy combined with longer life expectancy means that a typical married couple could be looking after four parents and up to eight grandparents"

While Europe may be looking to the future, in Japan the future has already arrived. The country has the oldest population in the world: 33% is over 60, 25% over 65 and 12.5% over 75. "Japan is very aged so the Government is prioritising making

cites age-friendly," says Setsuko Saya, head of regional policy at the OECD-led research into ageing in cities. Toyama, where 26% of residents are over 65, has adopted the principle of a compact city – which promotes high density, public transport, walking and cycling. The aim is to avoid the urban sprawl that can be so isolating for those with limited mobility. Despite being on a large area of flat land, which could be developed, the policy is not to expand outwards. A tram circles the city and investment is focused along the tramline and in the city centre, where there are public spaces for people to get together. People live in limited residential areas close to services and with good public transport – so they don't need to drive. Saya points out that it's important not to characterise ageing as a problem, and to recognise that these strategies don't just help older people: "The tram connects people as well as transports them. It's good for everyone."

While developing public transport is important, there will always be some unable to access it. A UK report by the International Longevity Centre found that despite transport being free for the over-65s, more than 30% of them don't use the service. In these cases, self-driving cars are put forward as a solution that could 'liberate' older people, as a mobility service for those who can no longer drive and are not served by public transport. Google are even "targeting" their self-driving cars to retirees. The city of Suzu in northern Japan has already been trialling the use of self-driving cars to keep older people mobile.

But how will these innovations work in an age of austerity, reduced pensions, later retirement and rising housing costs? Age-friendly design can help us rethink our cities, but how can we make sure these innovations reach the majority of older people? Looking to the future, with millennials expected to be poorer than their baby-boomer parents, young people unable to get on the housing ladder today are unlikely to have equity in old age. Professor Christopher Phillipson of Manchester University believes more political will is needed to make sure age-friendly cities include those hit

by austerity and industrial decline: "Age-friendly cities cost money but in the UK there is less money available for local authorities wanting to take action. There are considerable barriers – given pressures on budgets and limited commitment from policy-makers and developers. In the absence of these the possibility of creating age-friendly environments will be constrained."

"'Traditionally almshouses were set back behind a fence,' explains Witherford, 'but we wanted to create a version that would tackle the problem of isolation. It will have a lounge that opens directly on to the high street'"

In Manchester, the first UK city to be recognised as age-friendly by the World Health Organization, the Manchester Institute for Collaborative Research on Ageing (Micra) has been training older people to research what makes an age-friendly city. They found that for most people it was human contact, rather than high-tech gizmos that were important – such as door-to-door community visits for people unable to use public transport. "Manchester is age-friendly because it has strong political leadership and the city supports neighbourhood groups, and works with community leaders," continues Professor Phillipson. "The most important thing is collaboration across a broad range of interests, not least older people themselves."

25 April 2016

⇨ The above information is reprinted with kind permission from *The Guardian*. Please visit www.theguardian.com for further information.

Loneliness in older people

Older people are especially vulnerable to loneliness and social isolation – and it can have a serious effect on health. But there are ways to overcome loneliness, even if you live alone and find it hard to get out.

Hundreds of thousands of elderly people are lonely and cut off from society in this country, especially those over the age of 75.

According to Age UK, more than two million people in England over the age of 75 live alone, and more than a million older people say they go for over a month without speaking to a friend, neighbour or family member.

People can become socially isolated for a variety of reasons, such as getting older or weaker, no longer being the hub of their family, leaving the workplace, the deaths of spouses and friends, or through disability or illness.

Whatever the cause, it's shockingly easy to be left feeling alone and vulnerable, which can lead to depression and a serious decline in physical health and well-being.

Someone who is lonely probably also finds it hard to reach out. There is a stigma surrounding loneliness, and older people tend not to ask for help because they have too much pride.

It's important to remember loneliness can – and does – affect anyone, of any age. Here are ways for older people to connect with others and feel useful and appreciated again.

Smile, even if it feels hard

Grab every chance to smile at others or begin a conversation – for instance, with the cashier at the shop or the person next to you in the GP waiting room. If you're shy or not sure what to say, try asking people about themselves.

Invite friends for tea

If you're feeling down and alone, it's tempting to think nobody wants to visit you. But often friends, family and neighbours will appreciate receiving an invitation to come and spend some time with you.

If you would prefer for someone else to host, Contact the Elderly is a charity that holds regular free Sunday afternoon tea parties for people over the age of 75 who live alone. You will be collected from your home and driven to a volunteer host's home for the afternoon. Apply online or call Contact the Elderly on 0800 716 543.

Keep in touch by phone

Having a chat with a friend or relative over the phone can be the next best thing to being with them. Or you can call The Silver Line, a helpline for older people set up by Esther Rantzen, on 0800 4 70 80 90.

You can also call Independent Age on 0800 319 6789, Age UK on 0800 169 2081 or Friends of the Elderly on 020 7730 8263 to receive a weekly or fortnightly friendship call from a volunteer who enjoys talking to older people.

Community Network brings people together on the phone each week. To join or start a telephone group, call 020 7923 5250.

Learn to love computers

If your friends and family live far away, a good way to stay in touch, especially with grandchildren, is by using a personal computer or tablet (a handheld computer).

You can share emails and photos with family and friends, have free video chats using services such as Skype, FaceTime or Viber, and make new online 'friends' or reconnect with old friends on social media sites such as Facebook or Twitter and website forums.

A tablet computer can be especially useful if you can't get around very easily, as you can sit with it on your knee or close to hand and the screen is clear and bright. A sponge-tip stylus pen or speech recognition may help if

the touchscreen is difficult for arthritic hands or fingers with poor circulation.

Libraries and community centres often hold regular training courses for older people to learn basic computer skills – as well as being a good place to meet and spend time with others in their own right.

Local branches of Age UK run classes in computing to help older people get to grips with smartphones, tablet computers and email.

Get some tips and advice on how to become more confident using the Internet, including how to access your GP surgery online and how to look for reliable online health information.

You can find somewhere local to take free or low-cost computer courses through UK Online Centres.

Get involved in local community activities

These will vary according to where you live, but the chances are you'll have access to a singing or walking group, book clubs, bridge, bingo, quiz nights and faith groups.

Not to mention local branches of regional and national organisations that hold social events, such as the Women's Institute, Rotary, Contact the Elderly, and Brendoncare clubs in the south of England. The Silver Line helpline (0800 470 8090) can let you know what's going on in your local area.

Fill your diary

It can help you feel less lonely if you plan the week ahead and put things in your diary to look forward to each day, such as a walk in the park, going to a local coffee shop, library, sports centre, cinema or museum.

Independent Age has published a guide about what to do if you're feeling lonely, which includes tips about activities you could try. Download *If you're feeling lonely – how to stay connected in older age* (PDF, 2.97Mb) or order a free print copy by calling 0800 319 6789, or email advice@independentage.org.

Get out and about

Don't wait for people to come and see you – travel to visit them.

One advantage of being older is that public transport is better value. Local

---

---

bus travel is free for older people across England. The age at which you can apply for your free bus pass depends on when you were born and where you live. Contact your local authority for more information on how to apply.

Use the State Pension calculator to find out the exact date when you can apply for your free bus pass.

For longer distances, train and coach travel can be cheap, too, especially if you book in advance online and use a Senior Railcard.

The Royal Voluntary Service can put you in touch with volunteers who provide free transport for older people with mobility issues or who live in rural areas with limited public transport.

Help others

Use the knowledge and experience you've gained over a lifetime to give something back to your community. You'll get lots back in return, such as new skills and confidence – and, hopefully, some new friends, too.

There are endless volunteering opportunities that relish the qualities and skills of older people, such as patience, experience and calmness. Examples are Home-Start, Sure Start,

helping in a local charity shop or hospital, Citizens Advice, and school reading programmes.

Find out how to volunteer in your area on the Volunteering England website.

Read more about how to get started as a volunteer.

Join the University of the Third Age

The University of the Third Age (U3A) operates in many areas, offering older people the chance to learn or do something new.

Run by volunteers, U3A has no exams. Instead, it gives you the chance to do, play or learn something you may never have done before, or something you've not considered since your school days. U3A is also a great place to meet people and make new friends.

30 November 2015

⇨ The above information is reprinted with kind permission from NHS Choices. Please visit www.nhs.uk for further information.

© NHS Choices 2017

Here's why some Dutch university students are living in nursing homes

***An article from* The Conversation.**

THE CONVERSATION

By Johanna Harris, Senior Lecturer in English, University of Exeter

In today's society both young and old increasingly find themselves living in a bubble of like-minded and similar-aged peers. This is especially true of university students who leave home at 18 to live with people of the same age – who have quite often had similar life experiences.

Given this, the report that a Dutch nursing home has established a programme providing free rent to university students in exchange for 30 hours a month of their time "acting as neighbours" with their aged residents is unusual.

The programme has seen students in their early twenties sharing lives with residents in their eighties and nineties. As part of their volunteer agreement, the students also spend time teaching residents new skills – like how to email, use social media, Skype, and even graffiti art.

Reducing loneliness

The incentive behind Humanitas Deventer's 'exchange' programme is the research base that shows that reducing loneliness and social isolation improves well-being and extends life expectancy in the elderly.

And though research on the impact on students seems yet to be explored, from my own experience of running a similar project at the University of Exeter, I know that it is overwhelmingly positive – giving young people a sense of connection with older generations, and significantly increasing the likelihood that they will continue to volunteer after university.

Since 2011 student volunteers from the university's Department of English and Film donate their time to bring conversation, literature and friendship to the residents of over ten residential care homes across the city. And since the project's inception it is estimated that around 250 active volunteers have reached over 500 elderly residents – at least half of whom have dementia.

Reading between the lines

The Care Homes Reading Project draws upon the natural skill set of its target volunteer community – which includes a love of reading and an understanding of the power of literature to impact lives positively.

Research shows reading poetry with dementia sufferers – many who learned poetry by heart when they were younger – brings comfort and reassurance through hearing and reciting familiar verses.

Rhythm and rhyme bring a sense of order and predictability and, as this project has seen first hand, poetry can spark memories previously unknown to carers and even to family members.

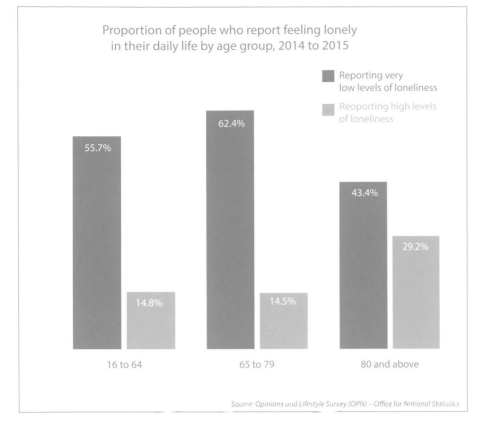

Proportion of people who report feeling lonely in their daily life by age group, 2014 to 2015

Reporting very low levels of loneliness

Reoporting high levels of loneliness

55.7%
14.8%
62.4%
14.5%
43.4%
29.2%

16 to 64
65 to 79
80 and above

Source: Opinions and Lifestyle Survey (OPN) – Office for National Statistics

Residents regain a sense of themselves as "a whole person, past and present", as one care home manager put it. And in one brilliant example, a 100-year-old resident found a shared play-reading session with one student volunteer revived long-buried leading-lady speeches once delivered when she was an actress.

"A Dutch nursing home has established a programme providing free rent to university students in exchange for 30 hours a month of their time 'acting as neighbours' with their aged residents"

Shared passions

Our experience in Exeter has shown that students can help to supplement the quality of care in homes by providing relief for overstretched staff. And residents typically respond with enthusiasm to the novelty of younger visitors and to the creativity students bring to their sessions.

Residents are also encouraged to be creative by writing their own poetry. And English students offer expertise in selecting and discussing appropriate literature, and show sensitivity to the emotional response that language can have.

Many students find the visits often evolve into wider-ranging conversations and discoveries of other activities that bring happiness and interest to the residents. One student now not only visits a care home to read but also to hold ballet classes. And in the same home other residents have made use of students' language skills, holding French and German conversation sessions.

Volunteer students look forward to their weekly visits. They find it is a space they can share poetry and stories – away from the demands of assessments. And many have said that it reminds them why they chose to study English literature in the first place.

Students also learn how past generations read the very same poems in surprisingly different ways. They see first hand how literature stays with us throughout life. And how the experience of shared reading helps to overcome the social and ideological disconnect between generations that plagues contemporary society.

Breaking boundaries

The moral health of a society is plainly visible in the way it treats its most vulnerable members, especially the aged. The Government recently announced that universities will be required to demonstrate their commitment to enhancing social mobility by establishing or supporting schools, so why not also mobilise the resources universities offer to enhance opportunity and well-being at the other end of life's spectrum?

"Research shows reading poetry with dementia sufferers – many who learned poetry by heart when they were younger – brings comfort and reassurance through hearing and reciting familiar verses"

The largest resource universities possess is the student body – a force with time, energy, few domestic responsibilities, and a desire to use their developing skills to make a positive difference in the local community.

Our reading project in care homes shows how both young and old can benefit from this type of arrangement. So just like the Dutch, it would be great if universities in the UK could also look to reduce the cost of tuition fees or accommodation in exchange for meaningful social investment to get more people young and old spending time together.

29 November 2016

⇨ The above information is reprinted with kind permission from *The Conversation*. Please visit www.theconversation.com for further information.

Designing housing to build companionship in later life

⇨ Exclusive polling finds London and the North West have the highest levels of loneliness amongst older people in the country, and Yorkshire the lowest

⇨ Over a million older people always or often feel lonely

⇨ Report finds a 'people and place' strategy is central to tackling isolation, and that redesigning 'cities for all ages' could help prevent social disengagement

⇨ Author recommends sociability, activities and sense of community found in retirement housing be used as a model in future housing provision

Loneliness in the older generation can be combatted through better housing design, building 'cities for all ages', and encouraging 'socialisers' to motivate outliers into activity, according to a new report published today.

The report – *Building Companionship: how better design can combat loneliness in later life* – was undertaken by cross-party think tank Demos with the support of McCarthy & Stone to better understand how loneliness amongst older people can be tackled. It comes amid growing concerns around isolation, with research for the report finding that those aged over 80 are almost twice as likely to report feeling lonely compared to their younger counterparts (14.8% of 16–64s report this, compared to 29.2% over the over-80s).

The report highlights wide regional variations in loneliness: Londoners aged 55+ report the highest levels, with four out of five (81%) feeling lonely at least some of the time, citing a lack of community spirit and support. In contrast, Yorkshire and Humberside emerged as the least lonely region, with 47% of over-55s saying they had not felt lonely at any point during the past 12 months, with local communities and neighbours playing a large role.

The impact of loneliness is significant and well documented – from poorer mental health to a greater risk of falling and hospitalisation. This, in turn, has obvious cost implications for the NHS, social care and the wider economy.

The report looked at the high levels of companionship found in retirement developments for lessons that could be learnt for how wider building design could address social isolation. It found that 85% of those surveyed in McCarthy & Stone developments said there is a good sense of community in their development, compared to just 51% of those aged 55+ in the wider community. What's more, those who live in retirement housing tend to report feeling much less lonely than their peers in mainstream housing.

The report recommends a number of lessons that can be applied from retirement housing to wider neighbourhood design, including:

⇨ Place: The creation of 'cities for all ages' – areas incorporating transport, housing, street furniture and green space which enable older people to remain socially, physically and mentally active. The report highlights small-scale schemes such as Gloucestershire Village and Community Agents, Rotherham Social Prescribing Scheme and Living Well Cornwall which help to address isolation among older people.

⇨ People: Local authorities should encourage active citizenship amongst the older generation, recruiting ambassadors to work with their peers to encourage social engagement and inclusion in the area. These ambassadors should also engage with private sector companies to help provide opportunities for socialising.

The report also recommends:

⇨ Increasing the provision of retirement housing: This is integral to the success of the fight against loneliness in older people given its many benefits. National and local

Total agreeing to the following statements	Whole population – all ages (n = 2,059)	55–64s (n = 297)	65–74s (n = 382)	75+ (n = 80)	McCarthy & Stone homeowners (n = 2,422)
There is a sense of community among the people who live in my housing development, neighbourhood or street	49%	42%	58%	51%	85%
I have made new friends and socialise more since moving into my apartment	–	–	–	–	70%
I have made new friends in the last 12 months	66%	51%	63%	56%	–
There are sufficient social events (for my age group)	38%	36%	53%	56%	73%
I have socialised very often with family or friends in the last 12 months	35%	33%	44%	46%	–

policy-makers are encouraged to help unlock supply and boost the development and availability of age appropriate housing for older people keen to downsize.

⇨ Neighbourhood planning strategies to have a Joint Strategic Needs Assessment and Health and Well-being Strategies to match. Statutory guidance should ensure loneliness is identified as a public health risk and as such needs to be tackled as part of health and care commissioning.

⇨ Real social networks: Schemes that develop older people's IT skills to prioritise education around activity which will result in 'real life' interactions such as joining forums and local groups.

Commenting on the report, co-author, Claudia Wood, Chief Executive of Demos, commented:

"This report provides an important evidence base on the role that people's surroundings play in shaping their levels of well-being, and is a wake-up call to an emerging crisis of loneliness and isolation amongst older people in the UK. As our population ages, there is no doubt that we need to urgently consider new approaches to the design of both public and private spaces, to ensure they are inclusive to older people, and encourage healthy, active and sociable lives. Our research makes the case that placing community connectedness and interaction at the heart of housing developments and urban planning could help to mitigate the substantial personal, economic and social costs posed by the increasing isolation of many older people."

Clive Fenton, CEO of McCarthy & Stone, the UK's leading retirement housebuilder, added:

"We supported this report to explore the extent to which older people are less lonely in retirement housing, and whether lessons might be learnt for wider aspects of housing policy, such as neighbourhood planning. The findings are compelling – our homeowners are typically much happier and better connected than their peers in the community. In turn, this delivers significant cost savings for the NHS, social care and wider economy due to the link between not feeling lonely and better health. But building more retirement housing is just one solution to combatting loneliness – developers and local and national government should review the recommendations in this report and consider adapting how we design neighbourhoods more generally."

12 April 2016

⇨ The above information is reprinted with kind permission from Demos. Please visit www.demos.co.uk for further information.

Internal 'clock' makes some people age faster and die younger – regardless of lifestyle

Study could explain why even with healthy lifestyles some people die younger than others, and raises future possibility of extending the human lifespan.

By Hannah Devlin

Scientists have found the most definitive evidence yet that some people are destined to age quicker and die younger than others – regardless of their lifestyle.

The findings could explain the seemingly random and unfair way that death is sometimes dealt out, and raise the intriguing future possibility of being able to extend the natural human lifespan.

"You get people who are vegan, sleep ten hours a day, have a low-stress job, and still end up dying young," said Steve Horvath, a biostatistician who led the research at the University of California, Los Angeles. "We've shown some people have a faster innate ageing rate."

A higher biological age, regardless of actual age, was consistently linked to an earlier death, the study found. For the 5% of the population who age fastest, this translated to a roughly 50% greater than average risk of death at any age.

Intriguingly, the biological changes linked to ageing are potentially reversible, raising the prospect of future treatments that could arrest the ageing process and extend the human lifespan.

"The great hope is that we find anti-ageing interventions that would slow your innate ageing rate," said Horvath. "This is an important milestone to realising this dream."

Horvath's ageing 'clock' relies on measuring subtle chemical changes, in which methyl compounds attach or detach from the genome without altering the underlying code of our DNA.

His team previously found that methyl levels at 353 specific sites on the genome rise and fall according to a very specific pattern as we age – and that the pattern is consistent across the population. The latest study, based on an analysis of blood samples from 13,000 people, showed that some people are propelled along life's biological tramlines much quicker than others – regardless of lifestyle.

"We see people aged 20 who are fast agers and we look at them 20 years later and they are still fast agers," said Horvath. "The big picture here is that this is an innate process."

The scientists found that known health indicators, such as smoking, blood pressure and weight, were still more valuable in predicting life expectancy in the 2,700 participants who had died since the study began, but that their underlying ageing rate also had a significant effect.

In a fictional example, the scientists compare two 60-year-old men, Peter, whose ageing rate ranks in the top 5% and Joe, whose rate is in the slowest 5%. If both are smokers and have stressful jobs, Peter is given a 75% chance of dying in the next ten years compared to a 46% chance for Joe.

This is not the first time that scientists have observed so-called epigenetic changes to the genome with age, but previously these were put down to wear-and-tear brought about by environmental factors, rather than indicating the ticking of an internal biological clock.

Wolf Reik, a professor of epigenetics at the University of Cambridge who was not involved in the work, said: "It now looks like you get a clock given to you when you're young. It gets wound up and the pace it's ticking at is dictated by this epigenetic machinery."

"I'm sure insurance companies are already quite interested in this kind of thing," he added.

> "You get people who are vegan, sleep ten hours a day, have a low-stress job, and still end up dying young"

Horvath said he has no plans to market the test, which costs around $300 per sample in his lab, but admits he has run his own blood through the analysis.

"I'm currently 48 and the test indicated I was 5 years older, which I wasn't too pleased about," he said, but adds that for an individual factors like blood pressure and smoking were more decisive. "My innate ageing rate is too fast to become a centenarian, but otherwise I'm not too worried about it."

The study, published in the journal *Aging*, suggests that accelerated ageing rather than simply a riskier lifestyle could explain why men die younger. Even by the age of five, Horvath said, the different speeds of aging between genders was apparent and by the age of 40 a biological age gap of one to two years opens up. "Women always age a little bit more slowly than men," he said. "It's not lifestyle it's this innate ageing process that favours women."

28 September 2016

⇨ The above information is reprinted with kind permission from *The Guardian*. Please visit www.theguardian.com for further information.

Mixing young and old people can extend lives

Research shows that developing relationships between the elderly and the young can be beneficial for the well-being of both parties.

By Ruth Wood

A lifetime of adventures as a cocktail bar tender, shipping company messenger and clerk in the Royal Artillery has given Paul Crowson many stories to tell. Young people love hearing how to make the perfect mojito, how he has travelled the world and how his wife was a professional chef in all the top hotels.

To tell these stories the 88-year-old has to get out and meet new people because he has no regular visitors and can no longer name a single neighbour in the north London apartment block where he has lived for 40 years. Friends and family? "They're all dead," says Mr Crowson, who had no children of his own.

His beloved wife Barbara died from cancer four years ago. "That was the worst thing that has ever happened to me. I didn't want to leave the flat at first but I got so lonely that in the end I had to go out and try to make something of my life," he says.

To overcome his loneliness Mr Crowson joined a weekly cooking club for budding chefs of all ages. The club, at Abbey Community Centre in Kilburn, is run by North London Cares, a community network set up to tackle isolation by running social activities that bring different generations together.

"I love coming here," says Mr Crowson. "We learn a new recipe every week and it gets me out and meeting interesting people instead of sitting at home looking at four walls all day. I was talking to a couple of students the other day. One of them had been to India and Dubai; another had just got a job in a film company. Young people really are adventurous and go-getters these days."

North London Cares is not a healthcare charity and makes no claims about keeping older people healthy or reducing the strain on GP surgeries and A&E departments. Yet a growing number of health professionals and researchers believe that's exactly what "intergenerational activities" like this can and do achieve.

Just as the harm caused by loneliness has been compared to smoking 15 cigarettes a day, the thinking now is that "age apartheid" can make us sick. Now new draft guidance from the National Institute for Health and Care Excellence (NICE), due to be finalised in November, says there is good evidence intergenerational activities improve health outcomes – and recommends all local authorities support and provide such schemes.

North London Cares has just celebrated its fourth birthday. Two-thirds of its older participants live alone and half are aged over 80 but the boroughs it covers – including Islington and Camden – are also full of high-flying young professionals from all over the world, with no roots, explains the charity's founder, Alex Smith. "Their older neighbours are often people who have lost their social connections in this rapidly-changing city but still have deep roots. They have so much to gain from hanging out together."

Intergenerational activities are of course nothing new – they are what good communities have always been about. However, with the rapidly ageing population, the globalised workforce, cuts to social care funding and an economic downturn, the traditional community has taken something of a battering, with some research showing that just five per cent of those over 65 have any form of structured contact with younger people.

"Over the last 50 years we have ended up with an apartheid between young and old," says Guy Robertson, a former Department of Health policy advisor on ageing and author of *How to Age Positively*. "We work and socialise in age-segregated worlds. It's not a healthy society."

Meeting older people is important for young people's long-term health too, he says. Research has found that our stereotypical view of ageing –

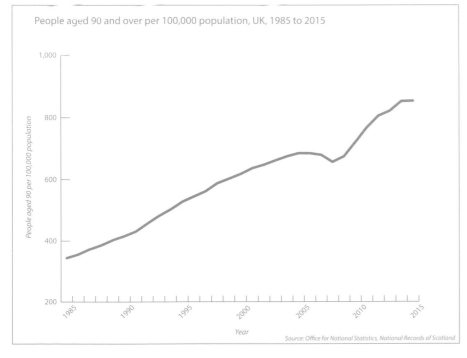

People aged 90 and over per 100,000 population, UK, 1985 to 2015

People aged 90 per 100,000 population

Year

Source: Office for National Statistics, National Records of Scotland

as a downward spiral of illness and loneliness – is formed early in life. If these views aren't challenged by mixing with older people, they become a self-fulfilling prophecy, leading to poor health outcomes. US research for example, has found that young and middle-aged adults who were pessimistic about getting old were twice as likely as optimists to suffer a heart attack or stroke within 30 years.

Millions of grandparents provide childcare and millions of middle-aged people look after their parents. But even if all British families decided tomorrow to live together and care for each other, it wouldn't be enough, say researchers: by 2017, the number of older people in need of care is predicted to outstrip the number of family members able to provide it, according to last year's *Generation Strain* report by the Institute for Public Policy Research. To contain the rising costs of health and social care, says the institute, we need to focus on keeping older people healthy by involving them in their communities.

It might sound like well-intentioned woolliness, except there is now good research to show that intergenerational activities have health benefits. The researchers behind the new NICE public health guidelines on independence and well-being in older people looked at examples around the world, especially Japan and North America, and agreed

there was consistent evidence that intergenerational schemes could save lives among older people, especially where participants were giving back to society.

Wales, Scotland and Northern Ireland already have government-backed, nationwide intergenerational strategies in place, although there is as yet no such nationwide strategy for England, where schemes tend to be patchy, small scale and run by arts and community organisations that are vulnerable to funding cuts and heavily reliant on lottery grants.

"Young and old people are great assets to each other and to their wider communities," says Alan Hatton-Yeo, founder of the UK's Centre for Intergenerational Practice, a charitable initiative set up in 2001. "We need to recognise the amazing potential that they have to contribute to society."

In the north London borough of Camden meanwhile, teenagers at Haverstock School have been socialising with their older neighbours for more than a decade, including involving local pensioners in tea dances, films and even drama productions. Molly Kutapan, 83, has appeared in three school plays and has loved every moment. "I've always wanted to go on stage, but I never got the chance at school," she says. "It's so much fun coming here and being with young people."

The grandmother-of-two, who was widowed in her 30s and lives alone, credited her visits to Haverstock School for keeping her fit, healthy and in good spirits.

"It's definitely made me more active," she says. "And it makes me happy. Sometimes it can get depressing in London. Everyone's in a rush; people don't know their neighbours. Some old people are depressed and on a lot of medication and sometimes they can go into themselves. It's good to spend a bit of time with young people and get their outlook on life. I always leave the school on a high and go home happy."

The sixth-formers benefit from the get-togethers too. Selin Sun started coming along to the social events when she was 14 and hasn't missed an event in four years.

"It's like a second family," says the 18-year-old, whose last surviving grandparent lives hundreds of miles away. "I used to be quite closed in, but I'll talk to anybody now, start a conversation at a bus stop or in the street. I'm much more confident."

23 August 2015

⇨ The above information is reprinted with kind permission from *The Telegraph*. Please visit www.telegraph.co.uk for further information.

Friends over 50 living together – a rising trend

Living with friends or housemates is a choice that housebuilders and policy-makers should make more widely available for the over-50s, according to a new study to be presented at the ESRC Festival of Social Science. Housing schemes offering this alternative approach – where people live independently but in shared communities – can reduce social isolation and allow people freedom as they age.

"More resources must be invested in helping the over-50s make informed choices about where and how they want to live in later life"

Andrea Jones from the University of Sussex has led research which demonstrates that schemes such as co-housing benefit people in later life in many ways. They enable members to remain active, continue contributing to community life and socially engaged into later life.

"Housebuilders and housing policy-makers need to wake up to the housing needs of the 'baby boomer' generation especially given the ageing population," says Ms Jones. "Increasing numbers of people post-parenthood are turning to schemes where they can live collaboratively with a community of people they share common values and aspirations with. Making these choices more widely available should be a priority for policy-makers so more people can benefit."

Communities owned and managed by householders are gaining in popularity in the UK. The aim of Ms Jones' research was to analyse the factors that make it possible in older age to live in planned residential schemes such as co-housing projects, housing co-operatives and ecovillages.

The ESRC-funded study *Alternative Capital, Friendship and Unspoken Reciprocity: what makes it possible to live in intentional communities into later life* is due to published in January. It is based on an analysis of nine communities in the South of England including Sussex and London, where individuals have chosen to live and often work together, in a shared house or on shared land such as cohousing schemes, housing co-operatives and ecovillages – these are known as intentional communities. Interviews were carried out with intentional community residents, who were asked about their housing choices.

Other research in this field identifies that women over 50, in particular, are choosing to live with friends in this way. These schemes are positive places in which to live, although community living is not easy and residents must be tolerant of other people's ways of doing things, according to the study.

The theme of later life housing is also explored in a separate study to be highlighted during the Festival. Sarah Hillcoat-Nallétamby from Swansea University has found that public services are too focused on encouraging older people to 'stay put' and age in homes which are often unsuitable for changing needs, instead of helping them plan ahead.

"Every person's home is their castle, and many fear the only option for moving elsewhere in later life (if needs be) is a Victorian-style institution," says Dr Hillcoat-Nallétamby from Swansea University's Centre for Ageing and Dementia Research. "It's partly by encouraging older people to think about their housing options that we'll stimulate property developers, landlords and local councils to be more creative and proactive in increasing the types of housing available for later life.

"More resources must be invested in helping the over-50s make informed choices about where and how they want to live in later life. We need to ask what they like and dislike about their current homes, whether they've been planning ahead in any way. All these questions get people thinking."

"Housebuilders and housing policy-makers need to wake up to the housing needs of the 'baby boomer' generation especially given the ageing population"

The research features interviews with older people given support in moving from home to an extra-care residence. Her findings are also based on an analysis of data from the 2004 Living in Wales survey covering more than 4,000 individuals aged 50 and above.

Both research studies will be highlighted at events as part of the ESRC's flagship annual Festival of Social Science. Andrea Jones will discuss her findings at an event called Age of Choice? Rethinking Life After 50 in Brighton for the general public. It will provide insights into retirement policies as well as the impact of ageist stereotypes on self-esteem.

Dr Hillcoat-Nallétamby's research will feature in the event Later Life Housing-Research and Information in Swansea. This is aimed at helping to inform people's thinking about their current accommodation, where they might like to live as they age and how they might realise their aspirations. The event will be run as a 'drop-by roadshow' for the general public, with researchers and service providers available throughout the day to respond to questions and provide information about housing options for later life.

3 November 2016

⇨ The above information is reprinted with kind permission from the Economic and Social Research Council. Please visit www.esrc.ac.uk for further information.

"Super-agers" may provide the secret to stopping memory loss in old age

Can we get them to find our car keys?

By Sophie Gallagher

Despite being nowhere near old enough to qualify for a bus pass, we are already starting to lose our memories.

But that is just an inevitable part of getting older, right? Well not for everyone.

A new study by Massachusetts General Hospital has revealed 'super agers' – a group of people who evade the seemingly inevitable fate of memory deterioration.

This remarkable phenomenon is leaving scientists perplexed as these elderly brains, which normally experience shrinkage over time, look like (and have key areas) which resemble much younger brains.

Author Alexandra Touroutoglou said: "We looked at a set of brain areas known as the default mode network, which has been associated with the ability to learn and remember new information, and found that those areas, particularly the hippocampus and medial prefrontal cortex, were thicker in super agers than in other older adults [who had experienced the anticipated shrinkage].

"In some cases, there was no difference in thickness between super agers and young adults."

The research, which was published in the *Journal of Neuroscience*, is the first step towards understanding how some lucky adults are able to retain youthful thinking and unusually resilient memories.

Touroutoglou said: "We desperately need to understand how some older adults are able to function very well into their seventh, eight, and ninth decades. This could provide important clues about how to prevent the decline in memory and thinking that accompanies ageing in most of us."

The trials were able to show that the size of these key areas of the brain were integral to retaining memory, and it is indeed the physical shrinkage that reduces memory recall for elderly people.

This new information will be integral in making important advances in preventing and treating age-related memory loss and various forms of dementia.

14 September 2016

⇨ The above information is reprinted with kind permission from The Huffington Post UK. Please visit www.huffingtonpost.co.uk for further information.

Good memories not key to older people's happiness

New research into the relationship between memory, identity and wellbeing in older people could lead to better support for people with dementia.

Changes in memory, as people grow older, can have a major impact on daily life and relationships with others. As well as forgetting simple day-to-day tasks, people can forget personal and life events.

"This type of memory – autobiographical memory – plays a central role in our sense of identity, and we wanted to explore how it would relate to well-being," explains Dr Clare Rathbone of Oxford Brookes University.

As part of this three-year study, researchers tested 32 younger and 32 older adults on their memory, sense of identity and well-being. Surprisingly, perhaps, findings show that general forgetfulness, a common experience among many older adults, is not related to well-being at all.

"Our results suggest that wellbeing in older age does not depend on what you remember, or even how good your memory is – what is crucial is how you conceptualise your identity in the present moment"

"Not being able to remember things or life events to the same extent as younger people didn't mean older people felt unhappier with life," Dr Rathbone points out. "Rather, we found that older people tended to be happier with their descriptions of 'who they were' and having a positive view of their self-image or identity was key to their well-being. Among younger people, the same relationship between identity and wellbeing did not occur."

When their memory performance was tested, younger participants in the study were able to remember more than older participants. But, interestingly, although older people scored less highly on memory tests, even when older people reported only very positive memories, this was not related to their general well-being.

"Our results suggest that well-being in older age does not depend on what you remember, or even how good your memory is – what is crucial is how you conceptualise your identity in the present moment," says Dr Rathbone.

These findings could, researchers suggest, pave the way for future research aimed at supporting well-being in people with very severe memory impairments and even dementia. "Having a sense of identity does not require complex memories for support," she says. "By finding new ways to help older people develop more positive views of themselves in the present moment it may be possible – despite memory loss – to support well-being in later life."

18 August 2016

⇨ The above information is reprinted with kind permission from the Economic and Social Research Council. Please visit www.esrc.ac.uk for further information.

Key facts

- Today, 901 million people are over 60. (page 1)

- 62% of people over 60 live in developing countries; by 2050 this number will have risen to 80%. (page 1)

- Over the last half century, life expectancy at birth has increased by almost 20 years. (page 1)

- It is estimated that by 2050 there will be over two billion people aged 60 and over, more than twice the number measured in 2000. Almost 400 million of them will be aged 80+. (page 1)

- 80% of older people in developing countries have no regular income. (page 1)

- Only one in four older people in low-and-middle-income countries receive a pension. (page 1)

- 26 million older people are affected by natural disasters every year. (page 1)

- The prevalence of disability among persons under 18 years is 5.8%; among 65- to 74-year-olds, the rate increases to 44.6%; the rate climbs to 84.2% among people aged 85 and over. (page 1)

- Nearly two-thirds of the 44.4 million people with dementia live in low- or middle-income countries. (page 1)

- A girl born in 2011 is expected to reach age 82.8; however, someone who was 60 years old already in 2011 was expected to live a further 25.2 years, that is until that are 85. (page 4)

- A newborn boy was expected to live to 40.2 in 1841, compared to 79.0 in 2011, whereas a baby girl was expected to live to 42.2 in 1841 and 82.8 in 2011. (page 4)

- Research from Royal London says an average earner who starts saving for an occupational pension at 22, and makes the minimum statutory contributions, would need to work until 77 if they want the sort of "gold standard" pension enjoyed by their parents. (page 7)

- A literature review conducted in Sweden in 2013 found a total of 33 studies across the world that explored views of death and dying among older people, although very few of these sought the views of the older old. (page 12)

- Within the Sandwich Generation, 71% of men say they maintain the well-being of their parents or their partner's parents compared to 65% of women. (page 13)

- Overall, 39 % of this generation say they've had to take time out of work to look after their parents, their partner's parents, or their children in the past 12 months. (page 13)

- 72% say they try to find activities that they, their parents and their children can do together. (page 13)

- 51% more people aged 65 and over in England in 2030 compared to 2010. (page 16)

- 101% more people aged 85 and over in England in 2030 compared to 2010. (page 16)

- By 2037, one in four of us will be over 65, compared to one in six at present. (page 24)

- Currently, retirement property makes up just two per cent of the UK's housing stock. Just one per cent of those in their 60s live in their retirement housing in the UK, compared to 17 per cent of the same age group in the United States. (page 24)

- By 2050, for the first time in human history, there will be more over-65s than children under 15. The number of people over 100 will increase by 1,000%. And as by then 70% of the world's population will likely live in cities, this will present huge challenges, and cities will need to adapt. (page 25)

- A UK report by the International Longevity Centre found that despite transport being free for the over-65s, more than 30% of them don't use the service. (page 27)

- 17% of older people are in contact with family, friends and neighbours less than once a week and 11% are in contact less than once a month. (page 29)

- 29.2% of people aged 80 and above report high levels of loneliness, compared with 14.8% of people aged 16 to 64. (page 31)

- 49% of people agreed that there was a sense of community among the people living in their housing development, neighbourhood or street. (page 33)

- 56% of people aged 75+ say they have made new friends in the last 12 months. (page 33)

- A higher biological age, regardless of actual age, is consistently linked to an earlier death. For the 5% of the population who age fastest, this translates to a roughly 50% greater than average risk of death at any age.

Ageing

As you got older your body wears out and experiences some changes. This can include the skin wrinkling and getting thinner, less body fat being stored and your bones and muscles becoming weaker. Your memory may also get worse as you age, and your immune system will not be able to fight disease as easily. This is because the cells in your body gradually become damaged and are no longer able to replace themselves. Although ageing can`t be avoided entirely, you can put off the effects of ageing by living a healthy lifestyle.

Ageism

The poor or unfair treatment of someone because of their age. Ageism can affect a person`s confidence, job prospects, financial situation and quality of life.

Ageing population

A population whose average age is rising. This can be caused by increased life expectancy, for example following significant medical advances, or by falling birth rates, for example due to the introduction of contraception. However, the higher the proportion of older people within a population, the lower the birth rate will become due to there being fewer people of childbearing age.

Alzheimer's disease

Alzheimer's disease is a form of dementia that affects the over 60s (most often, it is diagnosed in elderly people, although the rarer early-onset Alzheimer's can occur much earlier). There are more than 500,000 people affected in the UK. With Alzheimer's disease, the chemistry and structure of the brain changes, leading to the death of brain cells. As nerve cells in the brain are slowly destroyed, this results in memory loss (problems with short-term memory is usually the first noticeable sign) and difficulty in completing simple tasks. Prescription drugs can slow the progress of the disease. People with a history of heart disease, poor circulation and a family history of Alzheimer's are more likely to be affected. However, people who keep their brains active (such as doing crosswords and playing Sudoku) and have a diet high in Omega 3 (fish) are less likely to get Alzheimer's.

Centenarian

A person who has reached the age of 100. In the UK, the Queen sends out a special telegram to British citizens who celebrate their 100th birthday.

Dementia

Dementia is one of the main causes of disability in later life and mainly affects people over the age of 65. It can, however, affect younger people too; there are about 800,000 people in the UK with dementia, and of these over 17,000 people are under the age of 65. Symptoms of dementia include memory loss (particularly short-term, long-term memory generally remains quite good), mood changes (e.g. being more withdrawn) and communication problems.

Demographic changes (ageing population/grey population)

Demographics refer to the structure of a population. We are currently experiencing an increase in our ageing population. People are living longer thanks to advancements in medical treatment and care. Soon, the world will have more older people than children. This means that the need for long-term care is rising.

Osteoporosis

Osteoporosis is a disease that causes bones to become brittle and prone to breaking. One in two women and one in five men over the age of 50 will break a bone, mainly because of osteoporosis. As we grow older our bone density decreases. Weight bearing exercise and a diet rich in calcium and minerals help to strengthen bones and reduce fragility.

Pension

When someone reaches retirement age, they are entitled to receive a regular pension payment from the government. This payment takes the place of a salary. Many people choose to pay into a private pension fund throughout their career, in order to save extra money for when they retire. Often, employers also pay into a pension fund for their employees. The State Pension Age is gradually increasing. The Pensions Act 2011 will see the State Pension Age for both men and women increase to 66 by October 2020 to `keep pace with increases in longevity (people living longer)`.

Social care

Refers to non-medical care for the disabled, ill and elderly who find it difficult to look after themselves. Social care provides care, support and assistance to allow people to live their lives as fully as possible by helping them with everyday tasks they can`t do on their own. This allows people to take part in an active lifestyle as some people may need help to live in their home, get washed and dressed or go out and about to meet friends.

Assignments

Brainstorming

⇨ What is meant by the term 'ageing population'?

⇨ Why is our population ageing?

⇨ Is this a global issue or is it limited to the UK?

Research

⇨ Do some research to find out how people in another culture treat their elderly population. In particular you could look at Asian cultures such as the Japanese, where quality of life for retired citizens is said to be extremely high. When you have chosen your country and completed your research, create a PowerPoint presentation and share your findings with the rest of your class.

⇨ Create a budget for your retirement. Think about how much you will need per week for food, rent, bills and socialising. Then calculate how much you would need to save per month between now and when you retire in order to ensure you can live comfortably. Compare your calculations and figures with a friend's.

⇨ The article on page 20 suggests that brain training can improve memory and performance of everyday tasks in older people. Find out about ten of the best brain training apps available for smart devices such as tablets and phones. Make a list and jot down what each of the apps does. Now, in pairs, think about whether you could adapt any of these apps to 'real-life' training, for elderly people without access to apps. For example, if the key element of the game is problem solving you could create a task in which the participant has to sort physical objects into a particular pattern or order.

⇨ Do some research about care homes. You could try looking at care home websites, or even visit one if you have the chance. Perhaps you already know someone in a care home, maybe you could ask them about their experience? Do you think you would enjoy living in a care home? Maybe they are nicer than you thought they would be. Maybe they are worse. Write a blog post describing your feelings and thoughts about care homes.

Design

⇨ Choose an article from this book and create an illustration to accompany it.

⇨ Design a poster that illustrates the key statisitcs from page one.

⇨ Create a poster highlighting the key points from the article on page eight.

⇨ Design a 'retirement home of the future'. Think about the facilities you might need as you age, but make it fun as well as practical! Include a brief explanation of the features you have included.

⇨ Draw and describe a stereotypical old person. Compare your drawing with others and explain why you drew what you did. Now, draw and describe how you think people from an older generation see you. Look carefully at each drawing and discuss the idea of perceptions and stereotypes, and how these change with age. Is it harmful to discriminate against others because of their age?

Oral

⇨ Choose one of the illustrations from this book and, in pairs, discuss what you think the artist was trying to portray.

⇨ In small groups, discuss the things you might do to help an elderly neighbour who is extremely lonely.

⇨ Plan a lesson in which you will teach an older person who has never used a computer about the basics of the Internet. Remember things that come naturally to you, like switching it on (!), may be completely foreign to them, so think carefully about the steps you will need to cover. Also consider what this person might find the most useful about the computer and the Internet.

⇨ "Mixing young and old people can extend lives" – in small groups, discuss why this might be true.

⇨ Create a presentation to perform in front of your class, explaining what happens as you age.

Reading/writing

⇨ Write a definition of the term 'age discrimination'.

⇨ Write a letter from the point of view of someone at retirement age, explaining to a younger generation how important it is to plan for your retirement and think about finances and pensions.

⇨ Write a letter to the manager of a local retirement home, encouraging them to consider a scheme in which University or college students go to live in nursing homes. Read the article on pages 30 and 31 to get an idea of the benefits of the scheme.

Acknowledgements

The publisher is grateful for permission to reproduce the material in this book. While every care has been taken to trace and acknowledge copyright, the publisher tenders its apology for any accidental infringement or where copyright has proved untraceable. The publisher would be pleased to come to a suitable arrangement in any such case with the rightful owner.

Images

All images courtesy of iStock except the cover, and pages ii 1 and 15 © Pixabay.

Illustrations

Don Hatcher: pages 3 & 28. Simon Kneebone: pages 11 & 24. Angelo Madrid: pages 20 & 30.

Additional acknowledgements

Editorial on behalf of Independence Educational Publishers by Cara Acred.

With thanks to the Independence team: Mary Chapman, Sandra Dennis, Jackie Staines and Jan Sunderland.

Cara Acred

Cambridge, September 2017